Contents

Introduction

This workbook has been specially prepared to cover the essential
groundwork in English language teaching in preparation for the final
examination year and is designed to be used over a wide ability range.
It is intended as a supplement to the main work being done in lessons
and has the advantage that each exercise can be easily marked by the
students themselves, thus relieving teachers of the marking burden that
English usually imposes. This book takes the form of, for the most part,
double-page spreads, each being a series of exercises on one topic.
Most worksheets include a spelling section and often a section entitled
"Talking Points". The book is useful for homework exercises and in
final preparation for examinations. Sections on libraries and the use of
books, especially works of reference and encyclopaedias, are designed
to encourage students to use books more readily and read more widely.

1·Full·stops

Full-stops divide writing into sentences, which put some order into what is being said. They produce steps in the meaning so that a reader knows where one statement ends and another begins. You probably don't need to be reminded that sentences begin with a capital letter and end with a full-stop.

1.   Full-stops and capital letters have been omitted from the following sentences and it is obvious that, as a result, the meaning is less clear. Write out the sentences correctly, putting in the appropriate full-stops and capital letters.

a.   my main hobby is fishing my second hobby is collecting stamps

b.   the books in the cupboard were specially chosen for the project it had taken months to collect them from various libraries

c.   my father was standing in the doorway he looked at me as though I had done something wrong I looked at him as though I hadn't

d.   it was a big job to get the motor-bike in working order we spent all of Sunday and part of Monday morning on it

e.   when we arrived at the hostel the doors were closed we all grumbled and discussed what to do till opening time eventually Barbara suggested going to the local museum to see an exhibition of historical costumes

f.   tony kept his lead in the chess tournament that took place last week Harry was not on form and lost a number of games

g.   northern Scotland will be cloudy with some outbreaks of rain southern Scotland will have some sunny spells

h.   brittany has a long history of smuggling recently the emphasis has been on cigarettes and alcohol

i.   when we had finished the meal we went into the village to see the church it was quite late when we returned to the camp and all was in darkness

2.   Write out the following passages, putting in the necessary full-stops and capital letters.

a.   for our holiday we went to Marazion in Cornwall it was quite near Penzance and thirteen miles from Land's End we travelled all day and arrived at six o'clock in the evening having pitched our tent on a site called Weal Rodney, we went to see Land's End the next day we went across to St. Michael's Mount, which is about a quarter of a mile out to sea there is a causeway to it at low tide, but at high tide one has to cross by ferry the Mount is a parish of its own and is the smallest in Cornwall the weather was good there was no wind and it was sunny it was the beginning of a great holiday

b. in the coffee-shop they began talking about horse-riding "I remember once," said the Hodja, "that in my youth a man produced a horse that nobody had managed to break in as soon as anyone sat upon its back, it bucked so much that it sent him flying many of the young men in the village tried to mount it, but in vain finally, they asked me to try I was young and sturdy in those days I tucked up my skirts, rolled up my sleeves, grasped the horse by its mane and leapt on its back"

just at that moment a man who had been present on that occasion entered the coffee-shop

"yes, yes, go on," said the Hodja's friends, all agog

"it sent me flying," he said

c. peacocks have gone out of fashion now, except at the odd eccentric's dinner a young bird is worth the eating, however, if you get the chance, and tastes a little like pheasant, though a trifle more oily swans are still eaten once a year at an historical ceremony in the City of London the smoking-hot birds are brought into the dining hall in large pewter dishes carried by chefs, heralded by gaily-costumed musicians playing a traditional air all this beautiful decorative occasion cannot, however, alter the fact that the swan does not make good eating it is not only oily, but leathery too they'd be better off with a bit of chicken

d. it was my last year at school I was fifteen I thought it was a good idea to start something up like a cafe you get everybody taking an interest as they want refreshments and that's the only thing they didn't have there on the playground and you maka da money I said to Jim, my mate, "Let's build a cafe", so we did we worked together most of the time the first cafe we built was in an old caravan its tyres were all punctured, perished with age the second one was wooden we got all the shogwood off the builders and found some old doors and corrugated iron it got smashed too we got fed up we wanted to do something else

3. Having had some practice at punctuating other people's writing, you may be more aware of punctuation in your own. Choose one of the following titles for a short composition in which you pay particular attention to the full-stops that end sentences and the capital letters that begin them. a) This year at school. b) My week-end habits. c) Today's teenage fashions. d) The kind of music I like. e) What happened in this week's episode of a TV or radio serial. f) Escape to happiness.

Spelling group

bomb debt tomb plumber succumb subtle thumb comb
doubt numb

2·Commas(I)

Commas are used to divide a sentence into short units of meaning and they are particularly useful when a passage is being read aloud, since they indicate where the reader can pause. It would be difficult — and unnecessary — to give all the uses of the comma in written English, but we shall select a few of the more common uses and work at understanding those.

The comma is used to separate words or items in a list:
i.   We bought some shoes, hats, jerseys, ties and a scarf.
ii. He was a short, tubby, red-faced, comical young man.
iii. The wedding presents in the house included a toaster, a bed-spread, a carving set, a table lamp and a cookery book.

1. The following sentences are similar to the examples given above and contain lists of words or short phrases. Write out the sentences, putting in the correct punctuation. Note, however, that a comma is not placed before the 'and' at the end of the list.
a.   He decided to put the suitcases the tent the groundsheets the stove and the sleeping bags in the boot of the car.
b.   The gardener decided to plant marrows onions potatoes carrots and beetroot in his allotment this year.
c.   The attic was cluttered up with worn-out rugs broken chairs cracked crockery dust-laden sofas and heaps of old clothes.
d.   The car had advantages in speed comfort cost appearance and adaptability.
e.   It was the longest loudest silliest and most boring film I have ever had the misfortune to see.
f.   Mrs Treece was a smart elegant middle-aged lady and she turned up at the reception wearing a fabulous evening dress.
g.   The fete included stalls selling soft drinks used clothing children's toys articles made in the school drawings by the art students home-made jams second-hand books and lots of ordinary jumble.

The comma is also used to separate phrases which describe a series of actions and again there is no comma before the final 'and':
i.   Mr. Edwards strides into the wood, looks up into the tree, raises his gun to his shoulder, takes careful aim and fires.
ii. During the holiday we walked on the moors, swam in the river, visited an old castle, explored a disused quarry, fished for trout and did various jobs on the farm.
iii. He ran to the corner, leapt into a car and was soon away.

2. The following sentences, like those above, contain lists of actions. Write out the sentences, putting in the appropriate commas.

a. We knocked at the door called through the letter box rang the door-bell and shouted as loudly as we could to try to waken the sleepers.

b. Peel and slice the oranges arrange them in a shallow dish sprinkle with sugar and pour the juice over them.

c. The librarian noted down the title of the book walked over to the index cards looked through them carefully found the card he wanted and produced the book itself in no time at all.

d. Before leaving the house he turned off the electricity at the mains cut off the gas emptied the water tank secured all the windows double-locked the doors bolted the garden gate and left the key of the house with a neighbour in case of emergency.

e. My job in the supermarket was to check the stock on the shelves make a note of what was needed load up the trolley with replacements fix a price label to each item and fill up the shelves.

f. The photographer arranged us in our positions told us to relax and be natural returned to his camera squinted through the viewfinder said his final amusing remark to make everyone laugh and took the picture.

g. To train properly for any sport you should get an adequate amount of sleep each night take some exercise every morning before breakfast eat good food in moderate quantities avoid excessive smoking and drinking and attend practice sessions punctually and regularly.

h. My sister searched through the fashion magazine found the advertisement she was looking for quickly filled in the coupon for the dress got father to write a cheque for the amount to be paid posted the order that evening and had the new dress in time for the party at the week-end.

3. Write sentences in which you make use of a list of words or actions to describe:

a. the contents of a drawer or a handbag
b. the musical instruments in a group
c. the types of car at a rally
d. items in a school's clothing list
e. the actions of a player in a game before he or she scores a goal
f. the stages in preparing or cooking a simple dish
g. the actions of a head teacher on entering a hall to take assembly

Spelling group
wrangle   wrap   wrath   wreck   wrench   wretch   wring   wrinkle
wrist   playwright

3·Commas (II)

Three further uses of the comma are studied in this workpaper:

1. To enclose a short phrase that describes a word which precedes it in a sentence. For example:

Jimmy Lawton, the team manager, is a brilliant player himself.

The phrase *the team manager* describes *Jimmy Lawton* and is separated from the rest of the sentence by commas. The phrase could be omitted and the sentence would still make sense. It is said to be **in apposition** to the word or name that goes before it. Here are two more examples, with the phrase in apposition printed in italics:

i. Helen, *the new head girl*, was unexpectedly popular.
ii. We booked our holiday with Sky Tours, *the local travel agents*, and chose to go to Benidorm, *the resort in Spain*.

Now write out the following sentences, which contain examples of phrases in apposition, and insert the commas that are needed.

a. Julie Taylor the American folk singer appeared on television last night.
b. Ian Fleming the author of the James Bond stories used to live in this village.
c. He said his name was Captain Carlson the leader of the patrol.
d. I spoke to Mr. Gorton the curator of the gallery about the theft of the famous painting.
e. I the undersigned agree to abide by the conditions of the contract.
f. Mr. Eden Tanner the editor of the local newspaper and Mrs. Briggs the new mayoress were at the prize-giving ceremony.
g. 1939 the year the war began was the year I left Shotton the tiny Durham village and first journeyed south to London the most dangerous place in the country at the time.
h. The discussion panel consisted of Dr. Moore the well-known astronomer Dan Jacobson the South African writer and Mary Stott the journalist.

2. To mark off such words as *however, in fact, of course, therefore,* etc. For example:

i. We learned later, however, that the police had been informed.
ii. It seemed, therefore, that our report had been unnecessary.
iii. The house had, in fact, been sold several months before.

Now write out the following sentences, putting in the commas:

a. We shall of course do everything we can to help.
b. It was a question therefore of whether or not we were willing to pay the damages.

c.   After his jail sentence however we seldom ran into Kelly.

d.   "You are aware of course that the deposit cannot be refunded," said the house agent.

e.   I had not in fact passed any examinations in history, but I knew enough about the castle to act as a guide to the party.

3.   Where there is an obvious break in the flow of a sentence, forming a division between separate parts and where one would pause when reading:

i.   Since he knows the route, he ought to be the leader.

ii.   The craftsman, finding the conditions unsuitable, decided to leave the factory.

iii.   Whatever you do, don't get lost!

Decide where the division of meaning comes in the following sentences and write out the sentences with appropriate punctuation.

a.   Although the fire engines arrived immediately the fire was not put out till the early hours of the morning.

b.   The settlers discovering that the water supply was several miles away from their camp decided to move on.

c.   I don't know when we shall get there but I do know that it's going to take us a long time!

d.   The teacher finding that there was time to spare gave the class another set of problems to work out.

e.   No matter how difficult the conditions they were determined to cross the mountain in one day in spite of warnings against it.

4.   Write out these sentences, which need to be correctly punctuated:

a.   Bob Lennox the famous singer having retired from the world of pop decided to begin a new career in journalism.

b.   They were of course accustomed to trouble but were unprepared for the renewal of shooting since there was now an embargo on the import of arms into the country.

c.   He was known to a few people as Nick Williams but on the boxing circuit which he had worked since he was young he was known as 'Tiger Boy' the unbeatable champion.

d.   I am as you know a professional actor and my agent Derek Grouse will give you details of my experience in clubs films revues and straight plays.

e.   You may if you wish leave now but make it a firm decision for once taken it cannot be reversed.

Spelling group

science   conscience   scissors   unconscious   conscientious
crescendo   crescent   scent   incandescent   consciousness

4·Inverted commas (I)

When a sentence contains words which a person actually speaks, we use inverted commas or speech marks to show which words these are:
i.   The speaker said, "All helpers are needed!"
ii.   "It's very cold here," complained the old man.
The words in inverted commas are referred to as *direct speech*. There are several points to notice about the punctuation of sentences containing direct speech:

> There is a comma separating the direct speech from the rest of the sentence.
> The direct speech begins with a capital letter, even though it follows a comma.
> The final full-stop as in i). and the separating comma as in ii). come inside the inverted commas, as do exclamation and question marks.

1.   Write out the following sentences, putting in the necessary inverted commas, separating commas, full-stops and capital letters *wherever they have been omitted.*
a.   John said, We are all ready to go.
b.   The farmer shouted to the boys Get out of there!
c.   We ought to have left earlier, said Eileen, looking at her watch.
d.   The garden is lovely at this time of year remarked the guest.
e.   The nurse replied, we have moved the patient to another ward.
f.   There is no shortage of space in our house put in Mrs. Brown.
g.   You ought to have heard the din! laughed Robert.
h.   The landlady said eagerly there's an excellent view of the bay.
i.   The shop assistant replied, I'm sorry, we haven't that record in stock at present.
j.   I think we ought to protest about these dinners groaned Harry.

Very often the direct speech, though it consists of only one sentence, is split up into two parts:
"I thought I was late," he said, "but I'm glad to see that I'm not."
You will notice that each part of the direct speech is enclosed in inverted commas and that each is separated from the rest of the sentence by a comma.

> There are occasions, however, when the direct speech consists of more than one sentence and a full-stop and capital letter are needed:
>> "The supplies are urgently needed," said the commander. "Each of you has a special job to do."

If a speech contains two or more sentences that are of uninterrupted direct speech, then the inverted commas come at the beginning and the end of the speech, not after every sentence:

The manager said, "There are shop-lifters about. Be on your guard. Keep a sharp eye on suspicious-looking characters with big shopping bags."

2.   As in the first exercise, write out the following sentences, putting in the punctuation that has been omitted.

a.   "Is it true," I asked her, "that the flooding damaged your house"

b.   "It was an enjoyable day" said Len. We ought to go there again.

c.   You ought to know the way, Betty complained, you've been there often enough.

d.   In my opinion said the speaker, the taxation problem is crucial.

e.   What should be done about truancy asked the teacher.

f.   Ban all imports from the country exclaimed an angry man in the audience.

g.   "The young people of today" growled the octogenerian have it easier than we ever had. It's doing them no good, either.

h.   The animals are very well looked after here said the keeper. Our staff are fully trained in veterinary work. Would anyone care to ask any questions

i.   Did you watch last night's film on television? Brenda asked her friend on the bus next morning. It was terrific. I cried at the end. She paused and added, My dad thinks I'm too soft-hearted.

j.   We ought to leave Jan called out, before the roof starts caving in!

3.   Put your understanding of the punctuation of direct speech into practice by writing sentences based on the following:

a.   Fred expressing his admiration for Tom's new bicycle.

b.   Mavis asking her friend which pair of shoes she prefers.

c.   A teacher telling his class to be quiet.

d.   A lady in an art gallery saying that she admires the paintings by Constable.

e.   A hiker complaining that his pack is too heavy for him.

f.   The golfer saying that it is too wet to play golf today.

g.   Mrs. Smith explaining that she has to do the washing-up and then she will be able to go shopping.

h.   Bill not knowing which book to choose. He thinks both will be good.

i.   Grandfather telling us to look at the liner about to enter the harbour. He sailed in a liner like that one when he was a young man.

j.   The athletics coach raising the starting pistol and giving the three customary orders to start the race.

Spelling group

alter   altar   ascent   assent   baron   barren   bier   beer
councillor   counsellor

5. Inverted commas (II)

There are other uses of inverted commas besides that of enclosing direct speech:

1. To indicate in a sentence the title of a book, play, film, poem, painting, magazine etc. For example:
i. He said he had read "Gulliver's Travels" when he was at school.
ii. We saw "Orient Express" on television last night.
Write out the following sentences, putting inverted commas round the titles:
a. I borrowed Lord of the Rings from the school library.
b. We went to see Countess Dracula at the Odeon last night.
c. The class was reading The Red Pony last term and has begun To Kill a Mockingbird this term.
d. Dad says that when he was young he used to read Hotspur and Wizard, two of the most popular boys' weeklies.
e. I enjoyed reading Macbeth, but thought Macbeth himself a very unsympathetic character.
f. Of the Bond films I have seen, I preferred Dr. No to Goldfinger and Live and Let Die.
g. The programme named the school's most recent productions: Saint Joan, Journey's End and Oh, What a Lovely War.

2. A problem arises when a title occurs within direct speech. Inverted commas are needed for both and the usual solution is to use double inverted commas for the direct speech and single inverted commas for the title. For example:
i. "Did you see 'Jaws' last week at the cinema?" I was asked.
ii. "I thought 'Son of Superman' was terrific," Bill exclaimed.
Now write out the following sentences, putting double inverted commas round the direct speech and single inverted commas round the titles.
a. I didn't enjoy Westward the Wagons very much, said my aunt.
b. Have you seen Gone with the Wind yet? I asked her.
c. You left Jane Eyre out in the rain, complained my mother.
d. I would willingly lend you Frakenstein and What Katy Did — if I had them, said the warden, but unfortunately I have neither.
e. Watership Down was an immediate best-seller, said the librarian in her talk, but Shardik, by the same author, seems to have been less successful.
f. Take out Old Possum's Book of Practical Cats, said Miss Owen, the new English teacher, and start reading either Macavity, the Mystery Cat or Old Deuteronomy.

3. Inverted commas are sometimes called quotation marks because they are used to mark off a quotation in a sentence:

i. Stanley's most famous remark was "Dr. Livingstone, I presume".

ii. The repetition of the word "dark" creates a mysterious effect in the poem.

Note that in the first example the inverted commas come *before* the full-stop. Now spot the quotations in the following sentences and supply them with quotation marks.

a. In the new popular song you rhymes with blue and June rhymes with soon.

b. William fancied himself as an actor and went about the house declaiming, A horse, a horse, my kingdon for a horse.

c. One famous English writer said, Well, I've had a happy life — and died.

d. Jane was determined to appear polite and was continually saying I'm awfully sorry and I do apologise whenever she did anything wrong.

e. In the history quiz we were asked to name the persons who said We are not amused, Let them eat cake and Remove that bauble!

f. The poem's nautical style is developed with such phrases as gulls' way, running tide, rolling sea and a laughing fellow rover.

g. What a relief it was for Aunt May to hear Linda say I do when she had heard I won't so often.

h. The headmaster's most common phrase on entering a classroom was Please, don't get up, whereas the form tutor always said Stand!

4. Using the suggestions given below, write sentences which contain the appropriate inverted commas to mark off titles and quotations.

a. The last play or film you saw.

b. The last two books that have been read by the class.

c. The television serials you have enjoyed most.

d. A proverb that might be quoted frequently by one of your teachers.

e. Three words or phrases from a poem you have enjoyed.

f. The title of a book of poems and the names of two poems from it.

g. The catch-phrase of a popular comedian.

h. Four rhyming words from a popular song.

i. A well-known quotation from Shakespeare.

j. Some slang words in common use.

Spelling group
real   reel   nave   knave   idle   idol   lone   loan   dying   dyeing

6·Apostrophes

The apostrophe is used for three main purposes in English:
1. to show the omission of a letter or letters in a word;
2. to show possession;
3. to refer to letters and numbers in the plural.

We shall look at each of these in turn in this workpaper.

1. To show the omission of a letter in a verb:
i. when a verb is shortened: I am — I'm; you are — you're; he is — he's; it is — it's; they have — they've; will not — won't; they will — they'll; she would — she'd etc.
ii. when a particular pronunciation is intended: over — o'er; it is — 'tis; never — ne'er; of — o'; him — 'im; them — 'em; blowing— blowin'; here — 'ere; want — wan'; and — an', etc.

Now write out the following sentences, using apostrophes wherever it is appropriate:

a. They have come back home earlier than we expected.
b. We have got to go now, but we shall be back early tomorrow.
c. "I am sixty tomorrow," said my grandmother, "but I do not want any special celebrations."
d. It is time we gave up cards — we have been playing five hours!
e. I shall be along tomorrow to decorate, if you have got the paint.
f. You would think he would have written before now.
g. Tis a nasty night and there s a terrible wind blowin o er the hills.
h. Hes ad ard luck, I can tell you.
i. Ill give im what for if e comes ome ater ten o clock!
j. "Give em all youve got!" hed say. "Always leave em laughin."

2. To show possession:
i. 's is added to singular words to show possession, whether the words end in s or not: a boy's shoe; my friend's house; the ship's anchor; the ass's tail; the boss's daughter.
ii. 's is added to plural words to show possession only if they *do not* end in s: children's toys; the men's singles; women's clubs.
iii. to show possession in plural words which *do* end in s, an apostrophe *only* is added: ladies' singles; boys' games; ships' sirens; junior schools' competition; passengers' fares.
iv 's is used to show possession in such phrases as: one hour's time; six hours' work; four days' travel; yesterday's menu.

Write out the following sentences, putting in the apostrophes:

a. We all listened attentively to the professors lecture.
b. Johns school was built in the nineteenth century.

c.   In an hours time they intended to set off on a days hike.

d.   The mens singles championship was more exciting than the womens, though all the players lived up to Wimbledons high standards.

e.   There were six colleges taking part in this years county colleges chess tournament.

f.   One travellers wallet was stolen and two travellers passports were mislaid during the journey.

g.   A musicians technique does a great deal to develop an audiences appreciation of the composers quality.

3.   To refer to letters and numbers in the plural:

i.   Mind your p's and q's when you go to visit Aunt Harriet.

ii.   I had three 7's in my hand at the end of the game.

iii.   The group first became known in England in the 1960's.

4.   The following sentences contain examples of all the uses of apostrophes described in this workpaper. Write out the sentences, putting in the appropriate apostrophes.

a.   Theyve built several old peoples homes in our town since the 1950s.

b.   Didnt you know theyd offered Chelseas manager more money?

c.   She wont come earlier than six o clock, Im sure.

d.   Its time the dog had its food, dont you think?

e.   The years ending, the nights are darker and the winds whistle can be heard about the roofs.

f.   Weve always enjoyed the local Womens Institutes parties.

g.   I eard the feet on the gravel — the feet of the men what drill,
An I sez to my flutterin eart strings, I sez to em, "Peace, be still".

h.   "Remember," said the teacher, "that when you spell 'accommodation' you need two cs and two ms."

5.   Write out the following dialogue and put in the apostrophes needed:

Mother: I hope youve decided what to wear to tonights party, Teresa.

Teresa: Im not sure I have. Ive got so many things, havent I?

Mother: Youve got more than you need, certainly. Why dont you send some clothes to Oxfam? Other peoples needs are greater than ours.

Teresa: Ill look something out tomorrow. Heavens above, its eight o clock. Toms due to arrive in half an hours time.

Mother: Manys the time Ive wished youd be more punctual. Some boyfriends patience is more than I can believe.

Spelling group

pale   pail   root   route   which   witch   their   there   where   were

7·Colons and semi·colons

Two important punctuation marks that need to be studied are the colon and the semi-colon.

1. The colon is used to separate a general statement in a sentence from the details or explanation that follow it. Examples of its use:

i.   to introduce a list of related words or phrases:
The following people were present: the Mayor, the Town Clerk and several senior aldermen.

ii.   to introduce notes in tabulated form:
The causes of the revolution were: i). the social conditions; ii). the spread of new ideas; iii). discontent amongst the workers.

iii.   to introduce a quotation:
As Byron said: "Time, the avenger!"

iv.   After certain words such as: Telephone: Reference: Date:
Write out the following passages, putting in the necessary colons. All other punctuation marks have been included.

a.   The following trees were planted in the park firs, larches, oaks and several species of birch.

b.   The trains arrived at the times stated on the board 7.45 and 9.30.

c.   We can distinguish three main causes of the outbreak of the fire the dry weather, the timber structures, and the inhabitants' carelessness in disregarding elementary fire precautions.

d.   These I have loved
white plates and cups, clean-gleaming,
ringed with blue lines.

e.   The syllabus stated that two Communist revolutions were to be studied in close detail the Russian and the Chinese.

f.   His words rang out to the people "Get rid of this tyrant!"

g.   Applications are returnable to The Chief Officer, Kent County Council.

h.   There are two periods in one's life when the food one eats is important when it is drawing to a close and before it starts.

i.   Telegrams University, London. Ref. NR/244/75

j.   Country of origin Afghanistan. Part of plant eaten the root. Colour red, white or purple. Name of vegetable carrot.

2. The semi-colon is used to separate two or more statements in a sentence. These statements are often balanced one against another, or they form a series related to a main idea. The sentence requires a pause, but the full-stop would break up the flow and a comma would be too slight and might cause confusion with other commas. The solution is a semi-colon. Here are some examples of its use:

i.   A bicycle shed is a building; Lincoln Cathedral is a piece of architecture.

ii.   The report makes three main points: all front seat-belts should be the self-adjusting type; front-seat occupants should be made to wear belts; rear seat-belts should be a compulsory fitting.

iii.   On the beach that afternoon there were young toddlers busily digging holes and brandishing their spades at one another; tired mums and dads lying face-sunward in their deck-chairs; hardy youths who periodically raced across the sands and plunged headlong into the waves; pretty girls in fashionable bikinis; and hosts of others, all ages and sizes, all enjoying the luxury of a splendid summer's day.

Now write out the following passages, putting in the semi-colons.

a.   If the artist wishes to overawe me, I am ready to be impressed if he wants to construct a pattern, I will admire its beauty if he preaches, I am ready to be converted and if he wants to be of use to me, I shall be grateful.

b.   If a man will begin with certainties, he will end in doubts but if he will be content to begin with doubts, he shall end in certainties.

c.   We called at house after house we sang in courtyards and porches, outside windows, or in the damp gloom of hallways we heard voices from hidden rooms we smelt rich clothes and strange hot food we saw maids bearing in dishes or carrying away coffee-cups we received nuts, cakes, figs, preserved ginger, dates, cough-drops, and money but we never once saw our patrons.

d.   There were white-tusked wild males, with fallen leaves and nuts and twigs lying in the wrinkles of their necks and the folds of their ears fat, slow-footed she-elephants, with restless little pinky-black calves only three or four feet high running under their stomachs young elephants with their tusks just beginning to show, and very proud of them lanky, scraggy old-maid elephants, with their hollow, anxious faces and trunks like rough bark savage old bull-elephants, scarred from shoulder to flank with great weals and cuts of bygone fights, and the caked dirt of their solitary mud-baths dropping from their shoulders and there was one with a broken tusk and the marks of the full-stroke, the terrible drawing scrape, of a tiger's claws on his side.

e.   The reasonable man adapts himself to the world the unreasonable one persists in trying to adapt the world to himself.

Spelling group
possession   assassinate   committee   committed   succeed
accommodation   oppression   occurrence   address   embarrassment

8·Hyphens

The hyphen has many uses, but its main function is to join together words or syllables to form a single word-group. If the hyphen is omitted, the words are understood singly and this often changes the sense of the phrase. For instance, you might write about a "long lost friend", which could mean that your friend is both long and lost. What you really mean to say is that the friend is "long-lost". Similarly, if you wrote about "blue green glass" you might be thought to be contradicting yourself; but if you wrote "blue-green" your meaning would be that the colour was a shade that seemed to combine blue and green. In more detail, the hyphen is used:

i.   to link a short prefix to a word: pre-school education; anti-war demonstration; post-graduate studies; ex-policeman;
ii.   to provide a link between numbers and words: the Under-16 team; a 60-page report; and over-70's club;
iii. to represent a word that has been omitted: the 16-18 age-group;
iv.   to join separate words in the names of people and places: Jane Harrington-Smythe; Stow-on-the-Wold;
v.   to separate syllables in order to indicate a certain meaning or pronunciation: co-op (not coop); no-one (not noone); re-cover (not recover); re-count (not recount);
vi.   to link up the two parts of a word which occur on separate lines. The hyphen comes at the end of the line, after the first part of the word and the word should be hyphenated between syllables: mod-ern; endear-ing; excell-ent; care-fully.

1.   Write out the following phrases and add the hyphens:
      an old fashioned bookcase; the mid season cricket match; the under 20 foil competition; a tailor made suit; five three year old children; a one word answer; a never ending lane; tremendous self confidence; a non aggression pact; Newcastle under Lyme; after school activities; end of term disco; a five minute telephone call; a thick skinned person; to be caught red handed; hair raising adventures; it was an eye opener; a wild goose chase; a twentieth century novelist; the Tees side folk festival.

2.   Write out the sentences below and add appropriate hyphens.
a.   The ex captain of the Under 15 seven a side soccer team made an excellent end of season speech.
b.   The police officer described the ex criminal as a down at heel tick tack man of forty five.
c.   My brother in law manages the after sales division of the firm.

d. The play was rather far fetched and really more suitable for the under 5's than the over 14's.
e. The five man team made the award winning film in the North east.
f. We bought plenty of pre packed food to take with us on the hike.
g. Most of the perishable goods in the local co op were stamped with a sell by date.
h. The holiday brochure said the all in holidays were suitable for people aged 18 70 and that the week end trips were cheapest.
i. The rally contained both anti Communist right wing agitators and non violent middle of the road liberals.
j. John's end of term report commended his participation in out of school activities.

3. The following syllables or prefixes often form the first part of hyphenated words:
    sub   post   ante   anti   by   bye   ex   pan   semi   non
Place each of these before one of the words below to form hyphenated words:
    normal   natal   mortem   aircraft   directory   law   product
    African   detached   stick

4. Write sentences based on the suggestions below, each of which gives a clue to the introduction of hyphenated words:
a. a report given in the middle of the term;
b. the score of a match between your school and another school;
c. a political group that gets its title from being *against* something;
d. a political group that gets its title from being *for* something;
e. sentences in which you refer to one or more of the following imagined relations: your wife's mother, your daughter's husband, your second wife's son, your former wife;
f. the age of your father, your mother, your teacher;
g. an apprentice toolmaker works eight hours per day;
h. a chess team consisting of four members;
i. a revolt that lasted four days;
j. a project that was intended to raise funds;
k. a cycling tour that took you to various parts of the country.

Talking point
Look through newspapers and magazines and make a collection of hyphenated words. How many are newly-formed? What is the longest hyphenated word-group you can find?

Spelling group
rumour   glamour   humour   demeanour   valour   parlour
devour   scour   detour   candour

9·Dashes

There is often some confusion in distinguishing between the hyphen, which links words together, and the dash, which indicates a break in a sentence. Both are short lines, but they have completely different functions.

i.   The most common use of the dash is to break up a sentence into two parts, the second part commenting on the first:

> That's wrong — you ought to do it this way.
> They're very old — hundreds of years, in fact.

ii.   Then there is the dash which comes at the end of a statement to indicate that it is incomplete. This is frequently used in conversation or in dialogue when one person interrupts another or when a speaker is uncertain how to continue:

> "Surely you are not going to —," began Gerald.
> "I really ought not to tell you, but —," he hesitated.

iii.   There is the double dash which encloses (in a parenthesis) a statement which is not part of the main sentence. It is rather like an afterthought or an interruption which could be omitted without altering the flow of meaning.

> Lesley Kiernan — blonde and 16 years old — must surely be the most promising female athlete of the year.
> You will see the guards — beefeaters they're called — in their traditional uniforms.

iv.   Finally, there is the dash which is used for making notes, when there is neither the need nor the time for writing complete sentences, properly punctuated.

> Dinner in oven — must dash to evening class — back about nine — Love, Betty.
> Ivan IV — Terrible — first Russian ruler to assume title Czar — introduced Western ideas and culture into Russia — developed trade — country prospered.

1.   Write out the following sentences, which require the addition of a single dash:

a.   I'm sorry I had to leave I was called away urgently.
b.   Having a marvellous time weather very wet but it doesn't stop fun.
c.   It's extraordinary we've won!
d.   Your cricketers are tremendous always on top form.
e.   Never leave things lying around your own or other people's.
f.   You said something about the date that it was about ten years ago.
g.   You should have come earlier you've been told often enough.
h.   I can't believe it you weren't supposed to arrive for another week!

2. Write out the following sentences, putting in the necessary double dashes. Test the correct placing of the dashes by reading over the sentence and omitting the part between the dashes. The sentence should still make good sense.

a. This doesn't always or even usually happen.
b. We chopped down a number of trees ordinary pine trees and used them for the bridge we were making across the stream.
c. It required an effort of imagination the ability to put yourself into another person's place to appreciate the climbers' difficulties.
d. Whatever he was frightened of and I could see that he was frightened was something out of sight and hidden amongst the trees.
e. With his nearest challengers Torrance, Oosterhuis and Charles all making heavy weather of the course, Jacklin went ahead.
f. I am certainly well equipped if that is the right word for the trip.
g. I am concerned need I say it again? about the treatment of the boy.
h. He listened I felt it with profound attention and genuine interest.
i. I tried to conceal my surprise by heaven forgive me a gentle smile.
j. He was friendly with the famous or rather infamous highwaymen of his day.

3. Write out the following passages in note form, missing out words that are not essential to the meaning and replacing full-stops and commas by dashes:

a. I am in desperate need of more money. Please send some to my hotel. Prices are higher than I expected and I owe money to two shops.
b. Actors are sometimes called Thespians in honour of a Greek who lived over two thousand years ago. His name was Thespis, and he is said to have travelled round Greece with a company of strolling players and a wagon that could be converted into a stage.
c. In Manchester in August, 1819, a large crowd gathered to hear speeches demanding a change in the government's attitude to working conditions in factories. Soldiers were ordered to break up the meeting and in the panic which followed six people were killed and some four hundred injured. This tragic event happened in a large open space called St. Peter's Fields and it came to be known as 'Peterloo', a sarcastic reference to the battle of Waterloo.

Spelling group
meter   metre   pore   pour   precedent   president   principal
principle   stationary   stationery

10·Words from names

The next group of workpapers will aim at building up your vocabulary. It is possible to do this by absorbing new words from your reading, but there are hundreds of words, interesting in their origin and meaning, which you may never come across and the purpose of this and succeeding papers is to introduce you to some of them.

First, we shall look at words which are derived from the names of people, both real and mythical. Below is a list of men's names, followed by numbered sentences describing an important fact about each of these men. Pair off names and sentences, then write down after each number the word that is derived from the person's name.

Dr. Rudolf Diesel, Lord Cardigan, the Duke of Wellington, Lord Sandwich, Dr. Guillotin, Alessandro Volta, Monsieur Nicot, Count de Sade, Captain Lynch, Captain Boycott, Karl Marx, S.F.B. Morse, Dr. Silhouette, Dr. Mesmer, Dr. Bowdler, Louis Pasteur, Charles Macintosh, Duns Scotus, Don Quixote, Gabriel Fahrenheit.

1. An American captain who hanged people without trial in Virginia in 1776.
2. He devised a new method of sterilising milk.
3. He invented a type of oil-engine in which ignition of fuel is produced by the heat of air suddenly compressed.
4. He invented the electric battery and gave his name to a unit of electromotive force.
5. He censored Shakespeare's plays and cut out everything he thought vulgar or offensive to Victorian readers.
6. He was a great gambler and to avoid leaving the gaming tables for a meal, he ate his meat between two slices of bread whilst playing.
7. An Irish captain in the 19th century whom people refused to have any dealings with.
8. The first wearer — it is said — of a long-sleeved woollen jacket.
9. He gave his name to a machine for decapitating criminals during the French Revolution.
10. He first introduced tobacco into France.
11. He took a perverse pleasure in inflicting pain on others.
12. He wore knee length rubber boots during his military campaigns.
13. The philosopher who first formulated the ideas of Communism.
14. He invented a thermometer with 32° for freezing and 212° for boiling points.
15. An Austrian doctor who could hypnotize his patients into a state of immobility.
16. The inventor of a special telegraphic code.

17. The man who patented a coat made of special waterproof material
18. He produced portraits consisting of a shadow of the head only.
19. The Spanish character who did rash, impulsive, but noble deeds.
20. The 13th century philosopher whose teachings were ridiculed and whose followers were later called the Dunsmen.

The names of gods, goddesses, heroes and races of the Greek and Roman civilizations have been the origin of many words in English. Below are some to these names, with their definitions. Read the list, then write out the sentences that follow and insert in each blank a word that has been derived from one of the classical names. The names and the sentences are in the same order.

Mars, the Roman god of war; Bacchus, the Roman god of wine; Hypnos, the Greek god of sleep; Mercury, the winged messenger of the gods and famed for his speed; Hercules, the Greek hero renowned for his strength in overcoming great obstacles; Vulcan, the Roman god of fire; Narcissus, the boy in Greek legend who fell in love with his own reflection in a pool; Atlas, the mythical giant who bore the world on his shoulders; Tantalus, the Greek figure who was punished by having to stand chin-deep in water which receded each time he stooped to drink; Hygeia, Greek goddess of health

1. The band played some rousing . . . . music at the reunion of the regiment.
2. The empty wine bottles and beer cans suggested that the festival had been more like a . . . .
3. The trance-like state of the patient had been produced by . . . .
4. 'Quicksilver' is another name for . . . . because of its colour and the instability of its movement.
5. To build the house himself without professional help was an almost . . . . task.
6. The mechanic . . . . the tyre to repair the puncture.
7. The psychiatrist suggested that the patient's self-love was symptomatic of . . . . tendencies.
8. The . . . . had special maps to show changes in population.
9. To have the sweets on the top shelf, just out of reach, was very . . . . to the children.
10. The matron insisted on high standards of . . . . in the hospital.

Talking points
What is the classical origin of these words: cereal, vandalism, jovial, siren, draconian, January, July, August?

Spelling group
hoard   horde   main   mane   pier   peer   prophet   profit   vale   veil

11·Word-groups

Continuing the work on vocabulary, we shall look at certain words that fall into groups because they are related to a particular subject or because they have a prefix or a suffix in common. This workpaper is primarily an exercise in using a dictionary — so make sure there is one available before you begin.

1.　The word for a person who believes in a certain idea or who specialises in a certain subject often ends in *ist*. Can you match the words in **A** below with the appropriate definition **B**?

A　palaeontologist　criminologist　psychiatrist　trappist polygamist　ornithologist　numismatist　anthropologist philatelist　evangelist　psychologist　horticulturalist chiropodist　atheist　plagiarist

B　A person who: uses other people's ideas or writings and passes them off as his own; treats patients who suffer from mental illness; studies the workings of the human mind; preaches the gospels or is one of the gospel writers; cultivates gardens; collects postage stamps; marries more than one wife or husband at a time; claims that there is no God; collects coins; studies the development of man from his early origins; makes a study of crime; studies birds; is a member of a religious order that has taken a vow of silence; cures foot ailments; studies extinct animals.

2.　The prefix *ex* before a word comes from Latin and means *out* or *out of*. Each of the words in **A** below contains the idea of a movement 'out of' something. Can you match the words with their definitions in **B**?

A　excavate　excommunicate　exequies　exhale　exhume exonerate　expatriate　expire　expurgate　extricate　exude exodus　extradite　expedite　extrovert

B　to unearth by digging, particularly ancient remains; funeral rites; to give off a vapour or to breathe out; to censor or to remove objectionable matter from; to dig out, particularly a dead body; a departure of a body of people from a country; to disentangle, free or liberate; to ooze out or to give off a moisture, like sweat; to be excluded from membership of a church; to free a person from blame; a person who has left his native country to live elsewhere; to breathe one's last, to die; to return a criminal to his own country; to speed up; an outward-looking person, not self-obsessed.

3. Many words expressing a belief or an idea end in *ism*. Can you find a suitable definition of each of the following *isms?*
paganism   imperialism   patriotism   asceticism   chauvinism
Confucianism   occultism   hedonism   Quakerism   humanism

4. Words ending in *cide* are usually connected with death or murder (from the Latin *caedo - I kill*). Who or what is killed in:
suicide   insecticide   genocide   fratricide   regicide   patricide

5. Words ending in *crat* have to do with ruling or government (from the Greek *kratia — rule*). What kind of men are the following *crats?*
an aristocrat   a democrat   a bureaucrat   a plutocrat

6. *Poly* at the beginning of a word means *many*. Write brief definitions of the following *polys:*
polygon   polyglot   polymath   polytechnic   Polynesia
polychromatic   polytheism   polysyllabic   polyandry

7. *Anti* before a word carries the meaning *against*. Can you find out what the following *antis* mean?
anticyclone   antichrist   anticlimax   antiseptic   antisocial
antimacassar   antithesis   antidote   antipathy   antibody

8. Words ending in *graphy* always have some connection with writing (from the Greek *grapho — I write*). Find the meaning of:
bibliography   cartography   cardiography   lithography
radiography   seismography   hagiography   choreography

Talking points
a.   How does a biography differ from an autobiography?
b.   When would you consult an optician and when an occulist?
c.   What different opinions are held by an atheist and an agnostic?
d.   When would you go to a dentist and when to an orthodontist?
e.   How does an astronomer differ from an astrologer?
f.   What is the difference between the director and the producer of a film?
g.   How does a Anglophile differ from an Anglophobe?
h.   What do you think a Doctor of Philosophy is?
i.   What is the difference between an egoist and an egotist?
j.   Which is the defendant and which the plaintiff in a law case?

Spelling group
tobacco   accuracy   accustomed   accusation   access   accord
accumulate   desiccate   accelerate   piccolo

12·Words for people

The vocabulary on this workpaper deals with words we use to describe people, but not so much their appearance as their character, particularly when we pass judgment on them, either praising their good qualities or criticising their bad ones.

A. Imagine a party of twenty-five contrasting individuals, men and women, old and young. Below are two lists of sentences containing the name and the chief characteristic of each of the persons at the party. Write out the sentences in briefer form by using the appropriate adjective from the group that follows each list. For instance, the first sentence will read: Jack was unreliable.

1. Jack could never be trusted to do anything he promised.
2. Sam was full of his own opinions and would never see anyone else's point of view.
3. Mother wasn't mean, but she managed her housekeeping money very carefully.
4. Kim had a pleasant and agreeable manner.
5. Mavis looked pale, as though she had been unwell.
6. Karl was rude and offensive to everyone.
7. Peter was full of good humour and laughter.
8. Ken had had too much to drink.
9. Gordon always argued over the slightest thing.
10. Sally loved to talk about gruesome and horrific subjects.
    *morbid   intoxicated   thrifty   amiable   jovial   pallid
    ill-mannered   argumentative   unreliable   opinionated*

11. Henry was amusing and told some very funny stories.
12. Jane was wide-eyed and innocent and believed everything.
13. Grandpa was ninety and rather feeble-minded.
14. Sandra was shy and lacking in self-confidence.
15. Polly had forgotten to comb her hair and looked very untidy.
16. Uncle Bert was quite a character — full of odd little habits.
17. Doris tended to be stingy with her money.
18. Dad was tall, thin and somewhat bony in appearance.
19. Dave was a lazy type and loved an easy time.
20. Dr. Bray, like Bede, was old and worthy and respected by everyone.
21. Harry was awkward and tactless in company.
22. Pam tended to be sullen and moody.
23. Jock was always making bitter and critical remarks about people.
24. Ellen talked non-stop about the most trivial things.

25. Paula was extremely short-sighted.
    sarcastic   garrulous   unkempt   tight-fisted   indolent   droll
    venerable   gauche   naive   senile   diffident   eccentric
    gaunt   myopic   morose

B. This exercise in vocabulary could be called 'Twins', since it asks you to pick out two individuals who are similar in temperament. Read the following sentences and decide which two people — one from each column — could be paired off according to the adjectives that describe them. For instance, Mia is *pitiful* and Gary is *pathetic*.

Mia was pitiful	Vince was querulous
Billy was irritable	Gary was pathetic
Solomon was prodigal	Sue was obedient
Dirk was shifty	Percy was obdurate
Zeus was all-powerful	Eric was extravagant
Zena was submissive	Ben was evasive
Butch was loyal	Lee was energetic
Darrell was dynamic	God was omnipotent
Mick was stubborn	Harold was inefficient
Herbert was incompetent	Guy was faithful

C. Using the same idea, create a 'twin' for the following characters by finding a word in the dictionary similar to each of the words describing the characters below. Choose a name to go with the word and write out the matching sentences in pairs.

Kate was proud	May was fickle
Jake was ingenious	Sean was churlish
Len was quite contrite	Peter was industrious
Betty was irreproachable	Emma was stingy
Father was magnanimous	George was imposing
Dan was perfidious	Dorothy was malicious
Dick was infamous	Bernard was erudite

D. Create characters for whom the following words could be used, then write a sentence in which the word is explained, similar to the sentences in exercise A. For instance, for 'studious' you could write: 'Hamish was always studying books.'
    candid   hypocritical   gullible   curt   verbose   flamboyant

Spelling group
argumentative   jovial   eccentric   gaunt   dynamic   stubborn
irreproachable   temperate   hypocritical   studious

13·Words for things

A. Some people — ourselves included — can never think of the right word when they have to describe something technical. Usually a rather vague, roundabout description of the object has to suffice. Here are some of these attempts to describe objects connected with the house and garden. Write out each description and after it put the appropriate word, taken from the list below the sentences.

1. the timbers that support the roof of a house
2. the piece of wood that runs round the base of a wall in a room
3. the narrow piece of curtain along the top of the window
4. floors made up of little blocks of wood fitted together in a pattern
5. the right-angled pieces of metal for holding up shelves
6. nails that are coated with a silvery metal to prevent rusting
7. the cloth part of the settee or armchair
8. sacking you wrap round water pipes to prevent freezing in winter
9. the plaster or cement coating to outside walls
10. the pipe that lets water out when the tank is overflowing
   rafters   pelmet   skirting board   shelf brackets   galvanized nails   parquet flooring   upholstery   rendering   lagging overflow pipe

11. hinges that cause the door to rise when you open it
12. one of those electric sockets for taking two plugs
13. the board that runs round the house just below the guttering
14. the side of the house that goes up to a point at the roof
15. the mortar that fills up the joints and spaces between bricks
16. the strip of metal — usually lead — that covers the gap between the wall of a house and the roof of an attached garage
17. the timbers that run underneath the floor
18. the moulding that runs round the room where the wall meets the ceiling
19. the concrete post that supports the garden fence
20. the horizontal rails of a fence
21. the horizontal part of the stair
22. the vertical part of the stair
23. the tap on the pipe coming from the water tank which enables you to turn off the water supply
24. the part of the roof that overhangs the wall a little
25. the wooden framework of a door or window
   dual adaptor   fascia board   eaves   architrave   gable end rising-butt hinges   flashing   pointing   tread   joists   riser cove   spur   arris rail   stop cock

B. In this exercise the definitions are part of a church. Write out each one and add the appropriate word, taken from the list below.

1. the main part of the church, usually separated from the aisle by pillars
2. a reading desk or stand from which the lessons are read
3. the eastern part of the church, usually separated from the main part by a screen
4. a stone coffin or tomb often found in churches
5. a sculptured figure, often of a knight and his lady, reclining on the stone tomb
6. a small alcove or part of a church with its own altar
7. an underground cell or vault used as a burial-place
8. a projecting support, usually built on the outside wall of a church
9. the receptacle containing holy water used in baptism
10. the small room off the church in which the robes or vestments are kept

 lectern nave chancel chapel buttress vestry crypt
 font sarcophagus effigy

C. Write out your own definitions of the following words, all of which are associated with ships and sailing:

 starboard port hull bulwark hold keel tack aft
 capstan derrick rigging spar painter berth stern

D. Say briefly what occupation or activity you would expect the following types of room to be used for:

 galley keep cell green room refectory ward mess
 barn vault confessional morgue wardroom cellar
 dark room box office

E. There is an interesting 'technical' vocabulary associated with the kitchen also. Can you find a definition of the following terms used in cooking and say to what particular food, dish or drink they could be applied?

 to garnish to baste to marinade to sauté to souse
 to fillet to devil to grill to jug to ferment to parboil
 to emulsify to coddle to decant to broil

F. Still in the kitchen, but mainly French terms. Can you give an explanation of:

 purée fricassée eclairs millefeuilles meringue au gratin
 escalope hors d'oeuvre compote glacé bouquet garni
 vol au vent soufflé consommé croquettes

Spelling group
careful doubtful fruitful handful plentiful truthful
wonderful cupful restful sinful

14 · Proverbs

Proverbs are not as popular today as they were in Elizabethan and Victorian times when people were keen on spicing their conversation with wise sayings, many of which originated in the occupations and experience of the ordinary man. Yet the truths that are contained in proverbs are as relevant now as they were in the past and a few exercises might help to revive an old form of wisdom.

1. The first part of a proverb is in column **A**. Find the part that completes it from column **B**, then write out the complete proverb.

A	B
Do not carry your year's burden	in hammering cold iron
Separations are better	on one day
There is no purpose	ask him
Every stick	from malice
Look at the grain of pepper	than unhappy meetings
Call yourself unlucky	should not steal a minaret
No gnat stings	has two ends
Whoever has not first dug a well	and at the size of the sneeze
The best player of the game is the watcher	for the young may always grow wise
A young fool is better than an old one	if you take up coffin-making and people stop dying

2. The proverbs in **A** below are translations from other languages. Those in **B** are well-known English proverbs. Find those that correspond in meaning and write them down in pairs.

A   Wake not a sleeping lion.
A fox is not taken twice in the same snare.
An oak is not felled at one stroke.
Better small fish than an empty dish.
Stop up the crack or you will have to build a wall.
The strength of the hoe is tested in the ground.
One person can thread a needle better than two.
An old poacher makes the best keeper.
Take care what you say before a wall.
Idle brains are the devil's workshop.

B   A stitch in time saves nine.
The proof of the pudding is in the eating.
Walls have ears.
Set a thief to catch a thief.

Once bitten, twice shy.
Rome wasn't built in a day.
Half a loaf is better than none.
The devil makes work for idle hands.
Let sleeping dogs lie.
Too many cooks spoil the broth.

3.   Write down a simple explanation of the following proverbs:
Cheapest is dearest.
Liars should have good memories.
Spare the rod and spoil the child.
Those who live in glass houses shouldn't throw stones.
Every ass loves to hear himself bray.
Hunger is the best sauce.
It's an ill wind that blows nobody some good.
The darkest hour is nearest the dawn.
The habit does not make the monk.
Fling dirt enough and some will stick.
He who excuses himself accuses himself.
Do not look a gift horse in the mouth.
Hard cases make bad law.
Lend your money and lose your friend.
You cannot make a silk purse out of a sow's ear.

4.   What proverbs or sayings do you sometimes hear at home, used,
perhaps, by your parents or grandparents? Ask some older people if
they know of any that were popular in their day and make a collection
of proverbs that do not appear on this paper.

Talking points
Proverbs can often be contradictory. Discuss the following pairs of
proverbs and try to decide whether the truth lies in only one proverb or
in both.
Too many cooks spoil the broth. Many hands make light work.
Absence makes the heart grow fonder. Out of sight, out of mind.
What's done can't be undone. It's never too late to mend.
Look before you leap. He who hesitates is lost.
Do as I say, not as I do. Deeds, not words.
What must be, must be. Every man is the architect of his own fortune.
Call no man happy until he is dead. Life is sweet.
God preserve me from my friends. A friend in need is a friend indeed.

Spelling group
advertise   chastise   paralyse   compromise   devise   exercise
demise   supervise   surprise   improvise

15·Quotations

Below are a number of quotations on birds, animals and fishes. From the few essential details that are given, try to decide which creature is being described. When you have done this — and you will probably not get every one — you should look at the list at the end of the workpaper. It contains the names of all the creatures that are referred to in the quotations. Write down the list and by each name give the letter of the quotation that applies to it.

a. Four-legged, yet water-gifted, to outfish fish;
    With webbed feet and long ruddering tail
    And a round head like an old tomcat.

b. Twice you hear him call. Who
    is he looking for? You hear
    him hoovering over the floor
    of the wood.

c. It seems wrong that out of this bird,
    Black, bold, a suggestion of dark
    Places about it, there yet should come
    Such rich music.

d. Lazily through the clear
    Shallow and deep
    He oars his chartless way,
    Half-asleep,
    The little paradox — so bright — so cold,
    Although his flesh seems formed of fire and gold.

e. All suddenly mount
    And scatter, wheeling in great broken rings
    Upon their clamorous wings.

f. With white tails smoking free,
    Long streaming manes, and arching necks, they show
    Their kinship to the sisters of the sea —
    And forward hurl their thunderbolts of snow.

g. Black piper on an infinitesimal pipe.
    Little lumps that fly in air and have voices indefinite, wildly
        vindictive;
    Wings like bits of umbrella.

h. And trailed his yellow-brown slackness soft-bellied down, over the
   edge of the stone trough
And rested his throat on the stone bottom,
And where the water had dripped from the tap, in a small
   clearness
He sipped with his straight mouth,
Softly drank through his straight gums, into his slack long body,
Silently.

i. . . . . she wistfully, sensitively sniffs the air, and then turns, goes
   off in slow sad leaps.
On the long flat skis of her legs
Steered and propelled by that steel-strong snake of a tail.

j. He rises and begins to round
He drops the silver chain of sound,
Of many links without a break,
In chirrup, whistle, slur and shake,
All intervolved and spreading wide,
Like water-dimples down a tide.

k. He clasps the crag with crooked hands;
Close to the sun in lonely lands,
Ranged with the azure world, he stands.

The wrinkled sea beneath him crawls;
He watches from his mountain walls,
And like a thunderbolt he falls.

l. And though she doth but very softly go,
However, 'tis not fast, nor slow, but sure.

m. They keep together, the timid hearts;
And each one's fear with a panic thrill
Is passed to an hundred; and if one starts
In three seconds all are over the hill.

owl   otter   wild swans   blackbird   goldfish   bat   white horses
eagle   snake   gazelles   kangaroo   lark   snail

Your own writing
Choose an animal, a bird or a fish and in a few lines describe what each
is like — how it moves, what it look like, how it behaves. Try to bring
out the essential nature of the creature you are describing.

The following quotations are taken from a book of quotations and each
was found under a subject heading. Write out the quotations and after

each one put the heading you think it comes under, taken from the list at the beginning of each section.

1.   PATRIOTISM   TRAVEL   GRATITUDE   POVERTY MARRIAGE

a.   A man should know something of his own country, too, before he goes abroad.

b.   Never in the field of human conflict, was so much owed by so many to so few.

c.   With this ring I thee wed, with my body I thee worship, and with all my worldly goods I thee endow.

d.   To be poor and independent is very nearly an impossibility.

e.   Patriotism is not enough. I must have no hatred or bitterness to anyone. *(Edith Cavell)*

2.   MAN   POSSESSIONS   SPRING   TRUTHFULNESS   FAME

a.   For lo, the winter is past, the rain is over and gone; the flowers appear on the earth; the time of the singing of birds is come, and the voice of the turtle is heard in our land.

b.   Man, biologically considered, is the most formidable of all the beasts of prey, and, indeed, the only one that preys systematically on its own species.

c.   I would much rather men ask me why I have no statue than why I have one. *(Cato)*

d.   Paint me as I am. If you leave out the scars and wrinkles, I will not pay you a shilling. *(Oliver Cromwell)*

e.   He who says, what is mine is yours and what is yours is yours, is a saint. He who says, what is yours is mine and what is mine is mine, is a wicked man.

3.   TIME   SOCIAL JUSTICE   CHAUVINISM   SOLVENCY PEACE

a.   From each according to his abilities, to each according to his need.

b.   The years, like great black oxen, tread the world,
And God, the herdsman, goads them on behind.

c.   In proportion as the antagonism between the classes vanishes, the hostility of one nation to another will come to an end.

d.   Annual income twenty pounds, annual expenditure nineteen pounds nineteen and six, result: happiness. Annual income twenty pounds, annual expenditure twenty pounds ought and six, result: misery.

e.   How can what an Englishman believes be heresy? It is a contradiction in terms.

4. The following quotations are taken from Shakespeare
   DUSK SLAUGHTER COURAGE MODESTY
   INDIFFERENCE POISONING SNOBBERY
   OPPORTUNITY REPUTATION PRAYER

a. New widows howl, new orphans cry, new sorrows
   Strike heaven on the face.

b. The west yet glimmers with some streaks of day.
   Now spurs the lated traveller apace
   To gain the timely inn.

c.   Bespice a cup
   To give mine enemy a lasting wink.

d. The mind I sway by and the heart I bear
   Shall never sag with doubt nor shake with fear.

e. I will not choose what many men desire,
   Because I will not jump with common spirits
   And rank me with the barbarous multitude.

f. My words fly up, my thoughts remain below;
   Words without thoughts never to heaven go.

g. A maiden never bold: of spirit so still and quiet
   That her motion blush'd at herself.

h. There is a tide in the affairs of men
   Which, taken at the flood, leads on to fortune.

i. The patient dies while the physician sleeps;
   The orphan pines while the oppressor feeds;
   Justice is feasting while the widow weeps.

j. Who steals my purse steals trash;
   But he that filches from me my good name
   Robs me of that which not enriches him,
   And makes me poor indeed.

Talking points
Many of the quotations given in this workpaper are controversial and you may find yourself disagreeing with some of them. What have you to say about the following quotations? 1a,c,d,e; 2b,e; 3a,c,e.

Which of the quotations in this paper appeal to you a) because they seem to you to express a truth; and b) because they are very effectively written?

Discuss the meaning of the quotations 2c) and 2d) and say what impression you get of the characters of Cato and Oliver Cromwell from what they are reported to have said.

Spelling group
leisure heir weight height heifer sleigh rein feign neighbour neither

16 · Aphorisms

We often come across sayings in books that seem to sum up a great deal in a few words. They may express a truth with which most people can agree, or they may be witty sayings that merely sound as if they are true. They are similar to proverbs, but they have not got the universal popularity of proverbs and they tend to lie hidden in books until they graduate to a dictionary of quotations, along with the wisdom of famous men and women. When these sayings seem to be expressing a general truth they are called 'aphorisms'; when they are short, witty, but not necessarily true, they are called 'epigrams'.

1. Pair off the sayings in **A** with their explanations in **B**.

A
a. Necessity is the mother of invention.
b. Speak the truth sparingly, unless you want to live the life of a hermit.
c. The rule is jam tomorrow and jam yesterday, but never jam today.
d. There are only two families in the world, my old grandmother used to say, The Haves and the Have-Nots.
e. Wit is the salt of conversation, not the food.
f. Providence is always on the side of the big battalions.
g. I speak truth, not so much as I would, but as much as I dare; and I dare a little more as I grow older.
h. He is rich who hath enough to be charitable.
i. Some people think they can push themselves forward by patting themselves on the back.

B
a. The older one gets the more courage one has in speaking the truth.
b. A man who is able to give away even a little of his money to the needy should consider himself rich.
c. Benefits always seem to be in the past or in the future, but never in the present.
d. In war, the strongest armies always seem to have good fortune on their side.
e. When a need arises, man's ingenuity always finds a means of satisfying it.
f. All people can be divided into two groups: the rich and the poor.
g. Witty remarks can make a conversation lively, but they are no substitute for good, well-informed talk.
h. A person who is too frank will soon lose friends.
i. Certain people think that self-praise is the best way to get ahead.

2.   Each quotation below is followed by an explanation that may or may not be an accurate version of the original. If it is inaccurate, write your own correct version.

a.   Excessive severity misses its own aim.
Leniency produces better results than strictness.

b.   Nothing except a battle lost can be half so melancholy as a battle won.
It is even worse to win a battle than to lose one.

c.   The child is father to the man.
The character of the child determines what the character of the man will be.

d.   Use every man after his desert and who would 'scape whipping?
If everyone was judged according to his deeds, no one would be blameless.

e.   He that tells a secret is another man's servant.
To tell a secret is to do another person a service.

f.   Men do not realise how great a revenue economy is.
We do not realise how much taxation is made out of the economy.

g.   Revenge is a kind of wild justice.
To take revenge is a crude substitute for proper legal processes.

h.   The price of wisdom is above rubies.
You need more money to buy wisdom than to buy rubies.

i.   Liberty must be limited in order to be possessed.
True freedom can only exist where men submit to certain constraints.

j.   Men are not hanged for stealing horses, but that horses may not be stolen.
The aim of punishment is to deter the would-be criminal.

3.   Express in your own words the meaning of the following:

a.   The greater the power, the more dangerous the abuse.
b.   Prejudice is the child of ignorance.
c.   There was never a good war or a bad peace.
d.   Man's inhumanity to man makes countless thousands mourn.
e.   Nothing in excess.
f.   To spend too much time in studies is sloth.
g.   Speech was given to man to disguise his thoughts.
h.   Debt is the worst poverty.
i.   Friendship should not be all on one side.

Spelling group
psychology   psychiatry   psychologist   psychiatrist   psychic
psychedelic   psychotic   psycopath   psycotherapy   psychosomatic

17·Paragraph topics

Most writing in books and newspapers is divided into paragraphs. Why? Well, the paragraph is a sub-division of the main subject and it forms the basic structure of a piece of writing. This workpaper will be concerned with the structure of a single paragraph; later papers will deal with the development of paragraphs in a full composition and with the structure of paragraphs containing direct speech.

Because a paragraph deals with one topic, it often contains a statement that seems to sum up what the paragraph is about. This is called a topic sentence. It may occur anywhere in the paragraph, but it is usually found at the beginning and it acts as an introduction to what is to follow. For example:

Wood carving is almost certainly the oldest of the arts. The earliest craftsmen whittled wood with their primitive tools and carving has continued through the centuries to the present day. It is fitting that twentieth-century carvers should keep alive this ancient craft.

The topic sentence is the first sentence in the paragraph. It sums up the content of the paragraph, much as a newspaper headline sums up the contents of the article that follows it.

1. The paragraphs below contain topic sentences (not all of them at the beginning). Find these sentences and write them down.

a. Wood carving is an art and a craft. The carver who is primarily an artist will get opportunities for expressing himself while fashioning articles in the round, but the carver who is more interested in craftsmanship will get his reward from the skilful execution of a leaf or a scroll.

b. You can join a foot-slogging Everest trek to Katmandu, go plant-collecting on a mountain walk in Nepal, cross the Sahara by Land Rover, or make a magical but tricky trip across an Icelandic glacier. This travel agent specialises in real adventure.

c. It is not sufficient to renew a tap-washer occasionally, oil hinges when they squeak, or cover the walls with new paper in the spring. To keep a house in good order requires a methodical checkover at regular intervals. A house should be thoroughly inspected once a year and repairs dealt with in order of priority. This annual check should supplement brief inspections carried out at shorter intervals, say every three months.

d. I still recollect vividly my introduction to gardening. It was in 1915 or 1916 when I was no more than a small boy. My family, in common with tens of thousands of others, started to dig up the lawn and grow vegetables as our small answer to the U-boat menace. We were endowed with much enthusiasm and a complete lack of knowledge and I do not think our efforts were crowned with much success. But I do remember in the intervals of struggling with the unkindly London clay spending happy hours poring over the pages of Cousins' "Chemistry of the Garden" and H.H. Thomas's "Complete Gardener" and finding a new world of delight which has remained with me ever since.

e.   There is no doubt that profound and rapid changes in the world energy situation have occurred in recent years. Abundance of supplies has given way to relative scarcity. Market prices that have been stable have jumped upwards. Consumers accustomed to generous, if not wasteful, uses of energy are prevailed upon to limit their consumption. The major industrialised nations of the world find themselves increasingly dependent upon more expensive and less secure imports of energy.

f.   Remember that the centre of the stage is the most prominent spot. Use it to advantage. Different scenes in your play will bring different characters into prominence. Don't let them play their big scenes from bad stage positions. I am not suggesting that the principal player in each scene should be placed centre stage and left there; I am suggesting, however, that you pay particular attention to the placing of each character in his or her 'big moment'. It is often very difficult for a player to take control of a scene from a side position.

2.   Now attempt some paragraphs of your own, using topic sentences which you devise yourself or basing your paragraphs on those below. You will notice that the topic sentences suggest what the paragraph is to be about. For instance, paragraph a. will give some examples of changes that have recently occurred in soccer, paragraph b. will be a description of the best meal you have ever had and paragraph c. will list the career choices that were open to you.

a.   The game of soccer has undergone important changes in recent years.

b.   In short, it was the best meal I had ever eaten.

c.   The careers teacher told me that I had several choices open to me, but that I must choose before it was too late.

d.   There are several ways in which public transport can be improved.

e.   I considered that I had been very patient.

f.   It had been a day of disasters for all of the family.

g.   As to the clothes she was wearing — they were fantastic!

Spelling group

jealous   gorgeous   courageous   humorous   courteous
harmonious   conspicuous   impetuous   famous   hazardous

18 · Paragraphs in composition

A composition can be compared to a building and the paragraphs to the storeys of the building. Each storey deals with a different department of the same business, just as each paragraph deals with a different aspect of the main subject. A good example of the progression of a narrative through the paragraph structure is the passage below from 'Cider with Rosie', in which Laurie Lee describes episodes from his childhood and adolescence in a Gloucestershire village in the early part of this century. Read the passage and answer the questions on it.

The Parochial Church Tea and Annual Entertainment was the village's winter treat. It took place in the schoolroom, round about Twelfth Night, and cost us a shilling to go. The Tea was an orgy of communal gluttony, in which everyone took pains to eat more than his money's worth and the helpers ate more than the customers. The Entertainment which followed, home-produced and by lamplight, provided us with sufficient catch-phrases for a year.

Regularly, for a few weeks before the night, one witnessed the same scenes in our kitchen, the sisters sitting in various corners of the room, muttering secretly to themselves, smiling, nodding and making lah-di-dah gestures with a kind of intent and solitary madness. They were rehearsing their sketches for the Entertainment, which I found impossible not to learn too, so that I would be haunted for days by three nightmare monologues full of one-sided unanswered questions.

On the morning of the feast we got the school ready. We built a stage out of trestles and planks. Mr. Robinson was in the cloakroom slicing boiled ham, where he'd been for the last three days, and three giggling helpers were now forking the meat and slapping it into the sandwiches. Outside in the yard John Barraclough had arrived and set up his old field kitchen, had broken six hurdles across his knee and filled up the boiler with water. Laid out on the wall were thirty-five teapots, freshly washed and drying in the wind. The feast was preparing; and by carrying chairs, helping with the stage, and fetching water from the spring, Jack and I made ourselves sufficiently noticeable to earn a free ticket each.

Punctually at six, with big eating to be done, we returned to the lighted school. Villagers with lanterns streamed in from all quarters. We heard the bubbling of water in Barraclough's boiler, smelt the sweet wood smoke from his fire, saw his red face lit like a turnip lamp as he crouched to stoke up the flames.

We lined up in the cold, not noticing the cold, waiting for the doors to open. When they did, it was chins and boots and elbows, no queues, we just fought our way in. Lamplight and decorations had transformed the schoolroom from a prison into a banqueting hall. The long trestle-tables were patterned with food; fly-cake, brown buns, ham-sandwiches. The two stoves were roaring, reeking of coke. The helpers had their teapots charged. We sat down stiffly and gazed at the food; fidgeted, coughed and waited . . .

The stage-curtains parted to reveal the Squire, wearing a cloak and a deer-stalking hat. He cast his dim, wet eyes round the crowded room, then sighed and turned to go. Somebody whispered from behind the curtain; 'Bless me!' said the Squire, and came back.

'The Parochial Church Tea!' he began, then paused. 'Is with us again . . . I suggest. And Entertainment. Another year! Another year comes round! . . . When I see you all gathered together here — once more — when I see — when I think . . . And here you all are! When I see you here — as I'm sure you all are — once again . . . It comes to me, friends! — how time — how you — how all of us here — as it were . . .' His moustache was quivering, tears ran down his face, he groped for the curtains and left.

1. Give a suitable title to this passage.
2. What is the topic sentence of the first paragraph?
3. Paragraph 1 is a general introduction to the subject. Show that the following three paragraphs are about the stages leading up to the great event by quoting the key phrases or sentences from paragraphs 2,3 and 4.
4. In what way could paragraph 5 be considered the climax to the preceding paragraphs? In what sense is it *not* the climax?
5. Why do you think the part describing the appearance of the Squire is divided into two paragraphs?
6. Can you suggest what some further paragraphs might be about in order to round off this piece of writing? Give the topics of the paragraphs you would suggest.
7. From the speech the Squire makes, what do you think is implied about his character?
8. Find the meaning of the following words and phrases, according to their use in the passage:
   parochial   Twelfth Night   orgy   communal   intent
   monologues   transformed   reeking   catch-phrases

Spelling group
independent   transparent   experiment   sufficient   correspondent
fulfilment   permanent   treatment   confident   lenient

19·Preparation of a composition

You often have to write compositions in English. How do you prepare them? One way is simply to allow the thoughts to come into your mind and to write freely and spontaneously, without very much preparation. Another way is to make notes on your subject and to arrange your material in a logical order. Whichever way you choose, you will hardly be able to escape the need for paragraphs and you might find it helpful at the beginning to think of your subject in relation to the topic that each paragraph will contain. For instance, if you were to write on the subject "A Job Well Done", you might arrange the paragraphs as follows:

Paragraph 1 : How it came about that I was asked to do the job.

Paragraph 2 : How I set about preparing the work to be done.

Paragraph 3 : The job itself — the difficulties and the interest it presented.

Paragraph 4 : How the work progressed and was finally completed.

Paragraph 5 : What people said about it afterwards. The satisfaction, the reward or the disappointment. Intentions for the future. What I learnt from the experience.

This outline shows what structure the composition will take and it follows the development of the work itself. In fact, most titles suggest a paragraph development in themselves. You will, of course, introduce variations and new ideas during your composition and you may find either that you need more paragraphs than you planned or that some of your ideas cannot be filled out into paragraphs. You may find you want to devote a paragraph to an anecdote or narrative incident to illustrate your topic more effectively. However, you will at least have given some thought to your subject before plunging into the composition and your plan will be a useful guide.

1.   Below are some essay titles and by each one a list of the possible topics for the separate paragraphs. However, the topics are not in the correct order for the proper and logical development of the subject. Can you sort them out and write them down in the order in which they would most probably be used in the essay?

THE HOLIDAY

i.   the journey from home to your destination;

ii.   the day before leaving; packing problems;

iii.   journey home; stops on the way; conversations;

iv.   plans and booking; early discussions and choice;

v.   where we stayed; exploring the places nearby;

vi.   the best and worst days; the last night.

HOBBIES
i.   first efforts;
ii.   the search for a hobby; trying several unsuccessfully;
iii. purchase of tools and wood;
iv.   a wood carving book in the library interested me;
v.   what I attempted in my first carving; people's comments;
vi.   decision to go to craft college and take up carving.

GRANDAD
i.   as he is now; appearance, habits, speech;
ii.   his first job on leaving school and how much he earned;
iii. his travels abroad during the war; war anecdotes;
iv.   where he was born; details of his early childhood;
v.   setting up his own business and getting married after the war;
vi.   his relationship with his grandchildren;
vii. bringing up his own family.

PROGRESS OF A SPORTSMAN
i.   entering the County championships; a big match;
ii.   question of whether or not to become a professional;
iii. family discussions and other people's advice;
iv.   conclusion; the choice that was made and what it led to;
v.   playing the game for the first time as a child;
vi.   success at school; the encouragement of the sportsmaster.

2.   Now write some paragraph headings for the following composition titles. Make a list, similar to those in the exercise above, but putting the headings in the right order. Attempt to get some development in your essay, but treat your subject in any way you think suitable.
Sunday Morning
A day's good shopping
The night the television broke down
A troublesome evening at the club
A new member of the family
The experiment that went wrong
People I like and people I dislike
What ought to be done to improve our locality
Preparations for the big event
The beginnings of an interesting acquaintance

3.   Having prepared the outline of these essays, choose one title and write out the complete composition.

Spelling group
drought   bough   thought   through   rough   cough   ought
tough   plough   sought

20·Speech paragraphs

In the previous workpapers we dealt with paragraphs based on sub-divisions of a main subject. This workpaper will look at paragraphs based on direct speech. Look at the following example of writing which contains direct speech.

"Hello," said the instructor, "I thought you had given up swimming for this year." He sounded rather disappointed.

"No," I said, "I had to go away for a few weeks to visit some relatives in the North and I've only just returned."

"You'll have to put in a lot more practice, now that the season is well under way," said the instructor, "but if you turn up regularly, I think you'll make it."

"I hope so," I replied. "Anyway, I'll certainly do my best."

You will notice that there are four paragraphs in this piece of writing, one for each speaker in turn. The rule, therefore, is that you start a new paragraph when there is a change of speaker. The words not in direct speech are placed in the speech paragraph they are most closely related to. Remember also that when you begin a paragraph you begin about half an inch from the margin, but all succeeding lines in the same paragraph begin at the margin itself.

1.   The speeches in the following passages have been run together into one paragraph. Write them out in the correct form, starting a new paragraph for a new speaker and indenting a short space to begin.

a   "I think Brown will win. He's the best runner we have and he's been doing a lot of good training lately," said Harry. "You may think so," said Bill, "but he's got strong competition from at least three others in the race."

b.   "The clothes in the boutique were terribly expensive and I could find nothing I really liked," complained Jane to her friend. "Did you try the shops in Oxford Street?" Miranda asked her. "No, I hadn't time." "You should — there's always a better selection in the big stores and the prices are reasonable," said Miranda.

c.   "The plan won't work," said Drake grimly, "because there are too many guards on duty." "I don't agree," put in young Blake, then added, "because most of them go off duty at ten and only one or two are left to patrol." "It's been tried before — unsuccessfully," interrupted Scott, who was a pessimist, "and should not be tried again." There was a pause before Ainley spoke. "Well," he said coolly, "if we don't adopt the plan, what alternative is there?" "There are other possibilities," put in a new voice from the back.

d. "I met him on holiday in the South of France," said Margaret. "He was staying at the same hotel and we sometimes shared a table at meals." "Was he alone?" asked Winston, anxious to have as full a picture as possible of what had happened. "Quite alone," replied Margaret, "though he had an obvious gift of striking up friendships and he was seldom by himself." "Did he happen to strike up a friendship with you during the holiday?" asked Winston with a touch of concern in his voice. "More than that," Margaret said calmly. "He asked me to marry him."

e. "How much do you want for it?" Joe asked the dealer. "Five 'undred," the dealer replied. He was a shifty-looking youth who gave the impression that he was pushing up the price as high as he dared. "Five hundred for that banger?" chipped in Joe's wife, Alice. "It's dropping to bits!" "There's not a better bargain on the market than this, take my word for it." The dealer spoke with a confidence that required some effort. "What do you think, Alice? Shall we take the risk?" "Not on your life," said Alice. "I'd rather have a new washing machine than a dud car."

f. "That seals your fate," he said coldly. "You are very prompt in your actions, madame, but you have overdone it on this occasion." She threw the poker down with a clatter. "How hard you are," she cried. "May I tell you the whole story?" "I fancy I could tell it to you," said Holmes. "But you must look at it with my eyes, Mr. Holmes. You must realise it from the point of view of a woman who sees all her life's ambition about to be ruined. Is such a woman to be blamed if she protects herself?" "The original sin was yours." "Yes, yes, I admit it. He was a dear boy, Douglas, but he could not fit into my plans. He wanted marriage — marriage, Mr. Holmes, to a penniless commoner. He demanded money. It became intolerable. I had to make him realise it." "By hiring ruffians to beat him up?" "Well, I admit Barney and the boys were a little rough."

2. Using the paragraph structure for direct speech, write a conversation based on one of the following situations:
a. a group of assorted people waiting at a bus stop
b. three rebellious pupils planning an unauthorised day off school
c. a few members of a school team returning home after a match
d. a family arguing about which television programme to watch
e. a group of music fanatics at a festival.

Spelling group
usual   until   fulfil   enrol   enamel   barrel   bevel   sandal
pencil   alcohol

21· Summing up a list

There are times when it is necessary to speak or to write briefly, but accurately — to say what you have to say in as few words as possible, but making your meaning precise. This is a difficult thing to do because it requires clear thinking and a good command of language. To try to develop precise expression of meaning, the next group of workpapers will go into certain techniques that are eventually used in writing notes, summaries and a precis of an extended piece of writing. The first set of exercises on this theme will be to condense sentences or statements by replacing a group of words with a single word or short phrase which conveys the same meaning. Here are two examples in which the words printed in italics are replaced by shorter verbal equivalents:

i.   The shop window displayed *guitars, trumpets, oboes, flutes and drums.*
      The shop window displayed musical instruments.
ii.   Ellen was given *face-powder, lipstick, eye-shadow and foundation cream* on her birthday.
      Ellen was given make-up on her birthday.

1.   Write out the groups of words in a), then add the appropriate word or phrase that summarises each group, taken from b).

a.   cups, saucers, plates, dishes, mugs;
      cognac, whisky, gin and vodka;
      whales, dogs, bears, wolves;
      football, horse racing, cricket, ice hockey;
      rifles, shotguns, pistols, revolvers;
      a trunk, a suitcase, briefcase, hold-all and chest;
      rats, mice, voles, guinea pigs;
      members of the army, navy and air force;
      lockets, pins, brooches, rings, necklaces;
      agate, cornelian, lapis lazuli, rhinestone;

b.   spectator sports, crockery, spirits, semi-precious stones, rodents, mammals, luggage, firearms, servicemen, jewellery.

2.   What word or short phrase could be used to summarize the following?

a.   coca-cola, lemonade, orange squash, lemon barley water, fruit juice;
b.   empty cigarette packets, paper bags, old newspapers, sweet wrappers;
c.   oak, beech, mahogany, afromosia, teak and walnut;
d.   buses, trams, surface and underground trains;
e.   the potter, the cabinet maker, the carver and the weaver;

f.   nurseries, schools, technical colleges, institutes and universities;

g.   telephone, wireless, morse code, signals, the written word;

h.   strikes, lockouts, working to rule, banning overtime;

i.   the typewriter, the stencil cutter, the duplicating machine and the dictaphone;

j.   butterscotch, jelly babies, bars of chocolate and lollipops.

3.   Using the same method of summary, reduce the following sentences to the number of words shown in brackets.

a.   He gathered together his rod, lines, hooks, nets and bait. (6)

b.   Thousands of cars, lorries, scooters and motor bikes cross the bridge every day. (9)

c.   The airline also has flights to Malaya, Korea, Burma and Japan. (9)

d.   The woman was delighted with the wide shelves, the deep cupboards, extra drawers and the large wardrobes in the new house. (12)

e.   We saw only the high-jump, the shot-put, the javelin-throw and the long-jump at the school sports. (10)

f.   He had a special responsibility for the dictionaries, almanacs, directories and encyclopaedias in the school library. (13)

g.   Tennis courts, swing parks, putting greens and playing fields were within easy reach of the hotel. (9)

h.   Soup ladles, a mincer, a cutlery set and a fish slice were among the wedding presents. (7)

i.   He disapproved of bingo, the pools, betting on horses, and even of raffles. (4)

j.   His study included the arches, columns, buttresses, vaults and spires of the cathedrals built in the Middle Ages. (6)

4.   In the following longer passage the groups of words to be summarised are put in brackets. Find suitable substitutes for these word-groups, then write out the shortened version of the sentences.

There were some fascinating antiques for sale at the fair. I went immediately to the stall that sold (army badges, rank stripes, holsters, steel helmets and military uniforms) which I was collecting, whilst my father went to look for old-fashioned (electric cookers and fires, vacuum cleaners and wireless sets). As Karen was interested primarily in (painting, music, poetry and sculpture) and her brother, Leonard, had studied widely in (history, classical literature, modern languages and even geography), they made their way to the bookstalls.

Spelling group
bullet   jewellery   recollection   volley   umbrella   alliance
marvellous   illusion   parallel   collapse

22·Condensing a sentence

The second set of exercises in condensing a sentence shows that a long phrase or statement can often be replaced by a single word that conveys the same meaning. Here are two examples of sentences that can be condensed in this way:

i. He was a man *who always arrived on time.*
    He was a punctual man.
ii. Brian *always seemed to look on the depressing side of life.*
    Brian was a pessimist.

1. Rewrite the following sentences, replacing the words in italics by one of the following words: hypnotised, an heirloom, flattered, patriotic, ambidexterous, hybrid, solvent, octogenarian, nepotism.

a. Jane was often *praised with exaggerated compliments* by her friends.
b. The patient was *put into a dream-like state* for the operation.
c. The prime minister was accused of *showing undue favours to his relatives* when he was in office.
d. The specimens the laboratory produced were *a product of crossing two plants of different species.*
e. At last, after much work, he was *able to meet all his financial obligations.*
f. As an *old man who had reached eighty years of age*, he was given a special seat at the celebrations.
g. The soldier claimed to be *devoted to his native country.*
h. The Chinese vase was *passed down from generation to generation in the family.*
i. My father was *able to write with equal ease with his left and right hands.*

2. In order to replace a long statement by a single word, the structure of the sentence often has to be changed. Below you are given both the original sentence and the condensed version of it. Write out the condensed sentence, replacing the blank by a suitable word to convey the full meaning of the first sentence.

a. The church was repaired so that it looked as it did originally.
    The church was . . . .
b. The vase was so valuable that no price could be put on it.
    The vase was . . . .
c. He believed in doing good and helping people in need.
    He believed in being . . . .
d. They were always putting off the expedition to a later date.
    They were always . . . . the expedition.

e. His work was to make a list of the books on the library shelves.
His work was to . . . . the books on the library shelves.

f. The generations that come after us will have been greatly
influenced by the generations that have gone before us.
Our . . . . will have been greatly influenced by our
. . . .

g. He made attempt after attempt at the problem and never gave up.
He was a very . . . . man.

h. The atmosphere in the room was such that it was almost
impossible to breathe.
The room was . . . .

i. He was an actor who could play any part from comedy to tragedy
with equal skill.
He was a very . . . . actor.

3. Using the same method of compression, rewrite the following
sentences and reduce them to the number of words given in brackets.

a. The animal was capable of living on land as well as in the
water. (4)

b. The politician said he believed in the ordinary people being
allowed to elect their own representatives to parliament. (7)

c. The revolution caused the death of many titled men who owned
estates and had great wealth. (8)

d. Several of the children were unable to read or write and a few
were incapable of doing elementary number work. (11)

e. The director said that he was looking for a secretary who could
work quickly and accurately and who enjoyed mixing with other
people. (13)

f. The new boy began with an attitude of not caring one way or the
other. (9)

g. The manager was obliged to leave the firm because business had
slumped and there was practically no work for him to do. (5)

h. The suffragettes fought for the right of women to vote in
parliamentary elections. (8)

4. In the following passage the groups of words to be summarized are
placed in brackets. Rewrite the sentence in 26 words.
He (couldn't make up his mind) whether to stay in (the town
where he was born and bred) or to (leave England and settle
permanently in another country) and take with him (the money
his father had left him in his will) in order to set up a business
(that might bring in a lot of money).

Spelling group

commit   commotion   communion   comment   commerce
commander   commence   commonwealth   communism   commend

23·Omission of detail

You may often have to take down notes from a book or from a talk.
You cannot write down all the facts, so you select those that are most
important and leave out those that are comparatively unimportant.
Look at a sentence containing two statements of fact:

> The cycle race was held on the first Sunday in each month, though
> the date was often changed if the weather was bad.

The sentence falls into two parts, which are separated by the comma.
Which of these two parts is the more important? Obviously, the first
part is and your note or summary would leave out the second part.

Here is another example, with the divisions marking off the
separate statements:

> At the sale/ John bought a second-hand bicycle/ with the
> mudguards missing/ and an old record-player/ that needed a few
> repairs done to it.

You have to decide which of these facts could be omitted without
altering the essential meaning of the sentence. Opinions on selection
can differ, but your shorter version would probably read:

> At the sale John bought a second-hand bicycle and an old record
> player.

1.   In the following sentences the divisions have been indicated.
Decide which of the short statements you can omit and which you need
to keep. Write down the sentence summary.

a.   The parcel/ which was wrapped in ordinary brown paper/
     contained all the clothing he needed for the trip.
b.   Lawrence was studying horticulture/ as his main subject/ and
     forestry/ as his subsidiary.
c.   The artist/ who had lived in Chelsea for the past five years/
     specialised in painting portraits/ of well-known people/ such as
     politicians, actors, television personalities and writers.
d.   The people on the new estate complained that there were not
     enough recreation grounds/ particularly for the teenage
     population/ and that there were no social clubs/ either for the
     young or the old.
e.   The old ships,/ many of them cruisers which had done service
     during the war,/ were now in dry-dock/ awaiting repair or the
     scrapyard.
f.   Chris Finnegen,/ still sluggish after his recent defeats,/ retained his
     British light-heavyweight title last night/ at the Empire Pool,
     Wembley.

2. The next examples are taken from subjects in which you may be asked to take notes. Omit what is of minor importance and write down the essential facts, though you may have to alter the odd word here and there to make the sentence read properly. Some of the divisions are put in for you.

a. The two major events during the reign of George 111 were, first, the American War of Independence,/ when the colonists rebelled against unjust taxation and eventually freed themselves from British rule;/ and second, the French Revolution,/ when Louis XVI was executed and the Napoleonic era began.

b. There are many kinds of tortoise./ The most popular pet tortoise/ originated in the Mediterranean countries and/ is called the Greek tortoise./ It eats only vegetable food/ and particularly enjoys lettuce, cabbage, dandelion and clover./ In winter it hibernates/ and usually wakes up in the late spring./

c. Thomas Edison was an American inventor who made two of the most important inventions of modern times. He devised the electric light bulb, which soon supplanted oil and gas as a source of light; and he invented the gramaphone. He did not actually invent the telephone, but he helped to develop telephones and make them more widely used.

d. All daylight comes from the sun, which is 93,000,000 miles away. Think of that for a moment! Ninety-three thousand *thousand* miles! Light travels this enormous distance in about eight minutes, at the incredible speed of 186,000 miles a second.

e. With the development of railways many changes occurred in Britain. New factories sprang up near coalfields, though the conditions in them were far from satisfactory. New towns were rapidly built, most of them without a plan and seldom very beautiful. Ports were developed to deal with the increasing trade and Britain became one of the world's wealthiest nations.

f. There were many great achievements in the reign of Elizabeth 1, including the sea voyages of famous seamen such as Drake, Raleigh and Frobisher; the triumph over the Spanish; and the growth of the theatre, with such dramatists as Shakespeare, Marlow and Jonson bringing a new wealth of language into our literature.

g. At a special ceremony the President said that the space research programme had achieved all its objectives and he congratulated the astronauts on their magnificent achievement. He also announced that there would be a new attempt to explore the moon in the next decade.

Spelling group
pessimistic essential impossible harass issue permission
dissect dissimilar dissolve procession

24 · Minutes of a meeting

A common occasion for summarising is when minutes of a meeting have to be written. The writer has to convey the main points of what was said and to give an accurate account of any decisions that were made. His task is a difficult one because he has, of necessity, to omit a great deal of the discussion, yet avoid distortion through his omission. Moreover, he must convert the direct or actual speech of the meeting into indirect or reported speech in his writing. It is only when giving a verbatim account that a writer records exactly what was said, word for word, and this would be too lengthy a process for the taking of minutes.

Imagine a meeting of the local youth club committee. The members are John Barnes, Guy Holt, Lynn Parsons and Jill Tracy. Bill Sharples, the club leader, is the chairman. The discussion is on how to spend a donation of £30 which has recently been given to the club.

Bill: Well, John, you start off. How do you think we should spend the money?

John: I think we ought to use the money in decorating the club itself. The paintwork is really tatty outside and the main club room needs freshening up a bit. It looks shabby and nobody wants to come to a place that doesn't even look cheerful.

Guy: I don't agree. I think we ought to splash out and spend the money on a day's outing — to the coast or somewhere interesting. Decorating is routine stuff, we can do it any time. This money is special — we should spend it in a special way that will give the members some fun and enjoyment — show that the club exists to give them a good time.

Jill: It would be a pity to spend the money just on doing up the club. Besides, I think Mr. Martin, who left us the money, would have wanted all the club to enjoy it. An outing does at least make sure that everyone gets a share.

Bill: What do you think, Lynn?

Lynn: I can't decide. Why not split the money? Fifteen pounds on decorating materials and fifteen as a subsidy on a coach trip?

The minutes of the meeting might read like this:

The meeting was attended by . . . (give the names) . . . and was called to discuss how the donation of £30, given by Mr. Martin, should be spent. John Barnes suggested that the money should be spent on re-painting and decorating the club premises. Guy Holt disagreed and said he thought the money ought to go on a club outing, probably to the coast. Jill Tracy agreed with Guy and thought that most members would feel the benefit of an outing,

which is probably what Mr. Martin would have wanted. Lynn
Parsons suggested a compromise by splitting the money equally
between decorating and the outing.

Below is a further extract from the committee's discussions. Read it,
then write a minute on it.

Bill: Well, what shall we do with the new room we have got?

John: I think we ought to make it into a library or a reading room.
Some people want to be quiet and read when they come to the
club. Why shouldn't they have a special room?

Guy: How many bookworms have we? Three at the most! It would be
a waste of a good room to keep it reserved for a minority of
members.

Jill: A youth club is a place to meet other people. It should be really
sociable — not like a gentleman's club in London where you have
to talk in whispers all the time. I'm in favour of making the room
an extra coffee room where we could even serve suppers and
people could eat and chat.

John: Then we'd have all the problems of buying food, storing it,
cooking it and washing up! Who would want to do all the chores?

Lynn: Why not make it into a room for quiet games, like chess or
scrabble or bridge. It's best to have games like those away from
the noise and activity of the main club room. And it could still
be a reading room for those who wanted a quiet read.

Guy: I still disagree. How many want to play card games? Again, it
would become a room for a little clique who would then consider
it their own and would resent those going in who didn't play
cards or who didn't want to read.

Bill: What is your suggestion then? You don't seem to approve of
anything that has been put forward so far.

Guy: Well, what about a music room? For special sessions, I mean.
There's background music in the main club room, but this new
room could be used for anyone who wants to put on a programme of the music or the group he's particularly keen on. It
could be a sort of mini concert room.

Lynn: It's not a very large room and if you announce a record concert
by a very popular group you stand to have the room packed out.

Bill: Well, we have had four separate suggestions for the use of the
new room. We are obviously not going to agree on which one to
adopt. I propose that the whole subject be presented to a full
meeting of club members and that we ask them to decide.

Spelling group
excessive   progressive   passion   careless   incessant   confession
dissent   ambassador   necessary   assistant

25·Making notes

When you are writing notes on a subject, you will find that the techniques you have used for summary can be quite useful, particularly the omission of unimportant detail. However, notes do not always have to *omit* facts; facts can be retained, but arranged in a different way. Instead of writing in sentences, you can write short phrases; or you can arrange your material in tabulated form. In this way you will have notes that are simple, easily read and conveniently arranged for memorising.

The first passage below, for instance, is an account of the occupations and industries of various parts of America and it consists mainly of place-names or regions of the country and what is produced there. Can you write this passage in tabulated note form, making two parallel lists, the first giving the place and the second the corresponding products or occupations? The title of your notes could be 'Products of America' and you would begin:

south-east —— shipbuilding, steel rolling, coal mining, cloth-making, farming.

1. Shipbuilding, steel rolling, coal mining, cloth-making and farming are important in the south-east. Tobacco, cotton, peanuts, sweet potatoes and sugar cane are grown in the south. Oranges, lemons and grapefruit are produced in Florida, Texas and California. There are oil fields in the south-west. Vast cattle ranges stretch over the west. Fish, fruits and sugar come from the far-west; huge farms of wheat and corn occupy the middle-west. Motor cars are made near the Great Lakes; meat packing is done in the central states; iron is mined in the north-central area.

Using the same note-taking technique as for the first passage, write notes in list-form for the passage below. Choose a suitable title.

2. An orchestra is a group of musicians playing together on different instruments under the direction of a conductor. The stringed instruments carry most of the melody. They include the violins, violas, cellos and bass viols. The woodwinds, which are basically whistles, give a special colour to the music. They include flutes, piccolos and oboes. Then there are the brasses, the horn family, which are blown to reinforce the other instruments. They include horns, tubas, trumpets, cornets and trombones. The percussives are instruments which are struck in playing. The piano is the most familiar. Others are drums, timpani, cymbals and bells. The harp is sometimes used too.

Write notes on the following passages, using the tabulated or list form if you think it is suitable and omitting minor details that are not essential when giving only the gist of a subject.

3. Coal produces an incredible number of by-products, some of which are the following: tar, which is used extensively on roads; fertilisers, which are now used in vast quantities in large-scale agriculture; domestic articles such as soap, washing-powder and moth balls; paint, linoleum and dyes; nylon, which is now used for a vast range of manufactured goods; and — perhaps most surprising of all — aspirin, the most commonly used cure for headaches.

4. The architecture of the 19th century falls into three categories: Regency architecture, revival architecture, and what, for want of a better term, we shall call industrial architecture. The first belongs to the first thirty years of the century and is a direct continuation of the Georgian tradition of domestic building. The second overlaps the first in time and is a phenomenon peculiar to the 19th and early 20th centuries, a powerful movement for reviving past styles, of erecting buildings for all purposes in the manner of past ages. The third runs as an undertone to the other two throughout the 19th century, and continues in the 20th, and is the outcome of experiment with new building materials. In this category fall such buildings as the Crystal Palace, the iron and glass railway stations, and the bridges of Telford, Brunel and others.

5. The long, lithe body of the otter, ending in the long, tapering tail, is streamlined for swimming. The head is broad and flattened from above, the face short, the black eyes small but bright, and the short, rounded ears hairy. The ears are closed when under water. The legs are short and powerful, and all the feet are completely webbed. There are five toes on each, those on the forefeet having short pointed claws. The tail is somewhat flattened from the sides and forms a most efficient rudder. Below its thick base there is a pair of glands which secrete a most objectionable fluid. The fur is of two kinds: a fine, soft, waterproof underfur of whitish-grey with brown tips, among which are interspersed longer, thicker and glossy hairs, the so-called guard hairs. On the upper parts and the outer sides of the limbs, these longer hairs, which have a grey base, have rich brown ends; but on the cheeks, throat and underparts they are light brown to silver grey.

Spelling group
education   publication   qualification   demonstration
proclamation   reconciliation   deprivation   proportion   distortion
contortion

26·Addresses

Most of the writing you do when you leave school will be in the form
of correspondence. One very practical aspect of English, therefore, is to
study the rules and conventions relating to personal letters, business
letters, postcards and telegrams, and a most obvious starting point is to
look at names and addresses, since they are common to almost all
correspondence.

Names

A title goes before a person's name and it is usually abbreviated:
> Mr. (Mister); Mrs. (originally Mistress); Miss (unmarried woman or
> girl); Misses (plural of Miss); Ms (the female equivalent of Mr. and
> not declaring whether the woman is married or unmarried); Messrs
> (used for a business partnership, but not when that partnership is a
> Limited liability company); Esq. (Esquire, following the name and
> used as an alternative to Mr.); Mme (French, Madame);
> M. (French, Monsieur); Mlle (French, Mademoiselle).

It seems to be generally agreed that there is no full-stop after Miss,
Misses, Ms, Messrs, Mme and Mlle; and that there is one after Esq.
and M. The tendency now is to omit the stop after Mr. and Mrs. and the
Oxford dictionaries support this. However, there is still a school of
thought that would add the stops after these abbreviations.

1.   What abbreviations before a name would you use for the following
titles:
> Doctor, Professor, Reverend, Corporal, Sergeant, Captain,
> Flight-Lieutenant, Commander, Alderman, Councillor.

2.   Following the name and separated from it by a comma can come a
great variety of titles, awards, decorations, academic qualifications,
names of universities, etc. Find out what the following abbreviations
mean after a person's name:
> B.A., B.Sc., M.A., Ph.D., Oxon., Cantab., J.P., M.P., Hon. Sec.,
> Bart., Dip. Ed., L.R.A.M., O.B.E., M.B.E., D.S.O., R.N., D.B.E.,
> C.B.E., F.R.S., R.A.

3.   Write out the list of names below, adding full-stops, commas and
abbreviations where necessary:
> Mister James Brown, Henry Gordon Esquire, Mademoiselle
> Marie-Rose Legier, Doctor Grant Edwards, Professor Burgess
> N Wiseman Master of Arts Oxford, Sergeant William Perry Member
> of the British Empire, Kenneth Linden Esquire Member of
> Parliament, Messrs Smith Green and Gable, Miss Janet Arnold
> Justice of the Peace, Reverend A L Marshall Bachelor of Arts.

Addresses

If we take a typical family address:

78 Barford Drive, MATLOCK, Derbyshire. DE4 3BQ

we will note: the initial capital letters for the name of the street and the county; the name of the town written entirely in capitals; the capitals for the postal code, but no punctuation; the commas at the end of the first two lines and the full-stop after the name of the county.

4.   Write out the following addresses as in the example, putting in the appropriate punctuation and capital letters:

a.   62 mortimer street sandy bedfordshire

b.   78 forbes road barnet hertfordshire

c.   10 abbey lane abbey hill edinburgh EH8 8HL

d.   bridge estate speke road liverpool L24 9NQ

e.   70 yarm lane stockton-on-tees cleveland

5.   A great many abbreviations are used in writing addresses. Give the usual abbreviations for the words in **a.** and the complete word for the abbreviations in **b.**

a.   Avenue, Court, Buildings, Crescent, South-west, North-east, Gardens, Company, Limited, Brothers, Post Office Box, Number, care of, Great, On Her Majesty's Service.

b.   Wilts, Salop, Yorks, Hants, Herts, Notts, I.o.W., Beds, Worcs, Glam, Bucks, Staffs, Berks, Middx, Cambs.

6.   Putting together what has been learnt in this paper, write out the following names and addresses as they would appear on an envelope, using any abbreviations which you consider appropriate.

a.   James Danby Esquire 12 West View Road Hartlepool Cleveland TS24 0BN

b.   Mr J Healey Master of Arts Cambridge 4 Pine Lane Drimpton Beaminster Dorset DT8 3RJ

c.   Automobile Association Post Office Box 50 Basingstoke Hampshire

d.   The Furniture Contract Company Limited 188 Central Road Worcester Park Surrey KT4 8ED

e.   Mrs Elsie Parker BA LRAM Southern Music College Dover Avenue Southend on Sea SS99 6BB

7.   Write out in the form they would take on an envelope:

a.   your own name and address;

b.   the name and address of an adult at his place of work;

c.   the name of a teacher and his or her school address.

Spelling group

guarantee   guardian   guerilla   guidance   guilt   guillotine   guile
guarantor   guild   **guitar**

27·Personal letters

There are very few people who have never written a letter or who will never have to write one and as writing letters to friends, relatives and acquaintances is the only occasion on which most people express themselves in writing at all, it has a particular importance. Read the specimen letter below and the notes that follow it.

16 Brandon Crescent,
Wokingham,
Berkshire.

2nd June, 1982

Dear Harry,

It was a great pleasure to get your letter from Scotland and to read all about your travels there. I wish I could join you, but at present I'm up to my eyes in books — working away at examinations. I sometimes ask myself where all this so-called education is leading me, but then I start to daydream and waste hours — it's lovely! Still, it'll be over in a few weeks and then I shall hit the road, as you have done — probably to North Wales and the mountains.

Did you hear about Judy and the accident? She and Tom were involved in a motor-bike pile-up near the Pond's End roundabout last week-end. They're all right — fortunately they weren't going very fast — but it was a near thing and they were kept in hospital overnight with bruises and shock.

Your parents called in last Thursday and gave us a lot of news about you. No doubt they've told you all the local gossip, like the recent break-in at the youth club, the idea of having a camping holiday in September and (wait for it!) Bert Newley's sister winning the Miss Thames beauty competition. (She always was a bit wet!)

Still can't decide what to do next year — whether to leave school and get a job (assuming that some unsuspecting employer will have me) or to go back and become one of the sixth-form elite. Can you imagine me as a full prefect, lording it over the lesser mortals in the Lower School? I'll bet you can!

Will write more later when I have more time on my hands, and when I hear from you! Must get back to the grind now and hope that I don't grind to a halt. Don't get lost on those Scottish moors and keep off the whisky till you're old enough to take it like a man!

All the best,
Tim.

You will notice that:

i. The sender's address, but not his name, appears in the top right-hand corner of the note-paper. The address of the person receiving the letter is not included. A comma after 16 is optional.

ii. A space has been left between the address and the date, which is written slightly to the left. No comma after 2nd, but one before the year.

iii. The greeting (or salutation) begins at the margin and is followed by a comma. There are no rules about greetings in personal letters. You could begin: My dearest Sue, Hello there!, My dear Stuart,etc.

iv. Each paragragh is indented and is concerned with a separate topic.

v. The style of the letter is informal, typified by the frequent dashes, parentheses and exclamation marks.

vi. The signing-off (or subscription), like the salutation, is informal. You could write: Yours, Yours ever, All my love, etc. However, if you begin your letter with 'Dear Mr. Hayes' or 'Dear Miss Larkin' you would end with 'Yours sincerely', since the relationship is obviously not a close personal one. Note the capital letter for 'All' and the comma after 'best'.

vii. You sign with your first name or your full name, according to how well you know the person you are writing to.

1. Using the layout that is given opposite, write a personal letter on one of the topics given below:

a. To a friend who has recently left school and moved to a different town. Make your first paragraph an introductory one and in the remaining paragraphs write about three or four of the following: what you think about certain subjects and teachers; how the school has recently fared in sport; what you are planning for the next holiday; how some of your friends are getting on; how things are at home; when you hope to see your friend again.

b. From a young explorer in a remote region to his mother or father.

c. From a nurse or helper working in difficult flood or famine conditions abroad to an acquaintance at home.

d. From a criminal or a political prisoner in solitary confinement to a relative, friend or associate outside.

e. From yourself in an unusual place at an interesting time, to anyone.

f. From a mother or father to a member of the family who has gone abroad.

Spelling group
remittance   resemblance   remembrance   vengeance   assurance
deliverance   repentance   sustenance   tolerance   utterance

28·Business letters

The layout of a business letter is slightly different from that of a personal letter. The diagram on the opposite page illustrates the various parts, each of which is marked with a letter and corresponds to the notes given below. It must be remembered, however, that there are great variations in the layout of business letters and the example given here is simply one of them.

a.   The sender's address should be given in full (but not his name) and should be correctly punctuated. You may slope the lines or not, but make sure your last line doesn't run off the page.

b.   A line is usually missed between the address and the date, which should be written in the order: day, month, year. There are several ways of writing a date, but the most favoured is (for example): 20th December, 1982.

c.   Your own telephone number: not essential, but useful.

d.   A reference number should be given if you are replying to a letter that has contained one. In this case you would write: Your ref.: VR/TU/35 or whatever the reference was. If your own letter needs a reference number, this should be added underneath the previous one.

e.   Name and address of the person who is to receive the letter (the recipient) starts at the margin and is not sloped. It begins on the line below the date and is fully punctuated.

f.   The greeting or salutation begins at the margin with a capital letter and is followed by a comma. The general rule for salutations and subscriptions in business letters is as follows:

i.   an individual who is addressed by name: *Dear Miss Grant* or *Dear Mr Blake . . . . . . Yours sincerely*;

ii.   a person in an official capacity, or someone unknown to you: *Dear Sir* or *Dear Madam . . . . . . Yours faithfully* or *Yours truly*;

iii.   a company or partnership (Messrs): *Dear Sirs . . . . . . Yours faithfully*;

iv.   the editor of a newspaper: *Sir* or *Dear Sir . . . . . . Yours faithfully, Yours etc.*

g.   The first and all subsequent paragraphs are indented.

h.   Subscription begins about the centre of the page. It begins with a capital letter and is followed by a comma.

i.   Sender signs his name and either types it or writes it legibly underneath. Official title or position is also stated.

j.   An alternative to **e** for the recipient's name and address.

1.   What salutation would you use to begin letters to the following people, and how would you sign-off?

     Your Uncle Fred; your headmaster or headmistress; the editor of

c Tel. no.

a Sender's address

d References

b Date

e Name and address
of recipient

f Salutation
 g First paragraph begins _____

 g Second paragraph begins _____

h Subscription
 Signature
i Legible signature
 Title or position

j Name and address
of recipient
(Alternative to **e**)

the Daily Mail; the chief librarian, whose name you do not know; H.M. Inspector of Taxes; your form master or mistress; Messrs Lewis and Partners; the secretary of a club you wish to join; your neighbour; the manager of a hotel.

2.   Following the model of a business letter layout that is given on the previous page, write three letters, each on a separate sheet, using the following information:

a.   Your name is Thomas Gibson and you live at 23 Tipperary Road, Park Royal, London, N.W.10 6QP. You are writing to the Manager, Stereo Equipment, Ltd., 189 Stonebridge Road, Waddon, Croydon, Surrey, CR9 4DR and the date is today's date. Your letter should be in two paragraphs:

You bought a stereo assembly kit from Stereo Equipment last Saturday and discovered when you got the kit home that the bass control knob was the wrong size. You want to know if they will send you a replacement knob as soon as possible as you wish to use the player at a disco planned for the following week-end. You are enclosing the incorrect knob and would like one to fit model SE600. You would also like to buy a copy of 'Stereo Electronics', for which you are enclosing a 75p postal order, and would appreciate a free list of components on sale at the shop.

b.   Your name is Eileen Wallace and you live at 45 Northumberland Mansions, Waterloo Street, Newcastle-upon-Tyne, NE1 4DE. Your telephone number is Newcastle (0632) 20871. The date is today's date and you are writing to Mr J. Burtley, Site Manager of the Southern Riviera Caravan Park, Bournemouth, Hampshire. Your letter consists of three paragraphs:

You have read the advertisement in this week's 'Dalton's Weekly' and would like to know if the Bluebird 5-berth caravan, advertised at £80 per week in the high season, is available for the week beginning 10th August. If it is, what deposit would be required to book the caravan? You would also like to know if the amenities on the site include a swimming pool, a restaurant and a night club. As you do not know the area, you ask the manager if he can send you some information on places of interest in the district and whether there is a riding stable within easy reach of the site.

c.   Your name is Jonathan Selby and you live at 45 Hammond Street, Manchester M8 80G. You are writing to the Manager, Drake's Menswear Limited, Gofton Street, Manchester. The date is July 12th. Your letter is in four paragraphs:

You have read the advertisement in the 'Manchester Evening News' and would like to apply for the position of junior sales assistant (temporary). You are sixteen years old and a pupil of

Mountjoy High School. You have just taken C.S.E. examinations in Maths, Science, French and Music, and G.C.E. O-level exams in English Language, English Literature and History. You hope to return to school next term to take G.C.E. Advanced level, but would like to get temporary employment for about five weeks during the summer holiday. You have had some experience of working in a shop when you assisted in your brother's grocery business at Christmas and you occasionally served behind the counter at a newsagent's when you were a delivery boy. You will be free to start work on July 22nd and would appreciate having some details of the salary and proposed working hours. If the manager would like to interview you, you are free after four o'clock each weekday and all day Saturday.

3. Write a suitable business letter on one of the following topics, supplying a fictitious address of your own and a suitable business address for the recipient.

a. You are the secretary of the school's debating society and you write to the leader of one of your local political parties (a councillor or an alderman) to ask him if he will come to your school to address the debating society on the subject of Council procedure and debates.

b. You have received a statement of account from your local bank manager and you discover that a cheque drawn for £20 has been shown as £200 on the statement and as a result you appear to be seriously in the red. You point out the error and ask the manager to ensure that the correction will be made.

c. You are the father of a family who wishes to book accommodation in a hotel for two parents and three children. Ask for information and state your requirements.

4. Bring some examples of actual business letters to school and study how they differ from the 'standard' layout that is suggested here.

Read out some examples of letters to a newspaper. How do these letters differ from personal and business letters?

Spelling group
Rule: *i* before *e*, except after *c*, when the sound is *ee* (as in seen):
fierce   grief   mischief   shriek   relieve   yield   tier   field
receive   conceive   perceive   deceive   ceiling
Exceptions: weir   weird   seize   counterfeit   Sheila   Keith

29·Postcards and telegrams

A plain postcard usually conveys a short business message or a greeting — nothing too personal or confidential, since it can be read by anyone who sees it. Because the space is limited, some of the formalities of the ordinary letter are omitted:

i.   Your own address should appear in the top right-hand corner of the card only if you are writing a business message. It may be needed for reference or a reply. If the card contains a personal message, however, the address is often reduced to the name of the town only. The address of the person you are writing to does not appear on the correspondence side of the card.

ii.   The date is added, but often written in figures: 15/4/82.

iii.   You do not use a salutation, such as 'Dear Sir' or 'Dear Tom'.

iv.   You do not sign off with 'Yours faithfully' or 'Yours sincerely'. You simply write your first name if the card is personal and your full signature if the message is a business one.

A typical plain postcard with the message on one side and the address on the other would appear like this on the correspondence side:

67, Green Lane
Morden
Surrey
6/5/82

I have read your advertisement in the Wimbledon Borough News and would be pleased if you would send me a free copy of 'Start Your Own Pop Group'
E.L.Mason

The correspondence side of a picture postcard would be like this:

Southend-on-Sea
Sunday

SHRIMP
POSTCARD

Arrived in downpour and got soaking wet looking for hotel. Closed! Staff on strike! Slept in shelter on promenade — Wind moderate to gale force. Wish you were here. Money running short and five days to go. Don't forget to feed the rabbits
Harry.

Mrs J. Smithies,
32 St. Joans Ave.,
SALISBURY,
Wilts.

1. Using about ten lines of an exercise book to represent the correspondence side of a plain postcard, write postcards:
a. requesting your local librarian to reserve you a copy of 'Birds of the Wilderness' by James Freeman when it is published;
b. asking a travel agent in your town to send you the latest brochures on summer holidays in Spain and Portugal;
c. to the captain of a school hockey or soccer team confirming your acceptance of a particular fixture;
d. to a dentist, apologising for having to cancel an appointment.

2. Using about ten lines to represent the correspondence side of a picture postcard, write:
a. a card from yourself to your parents, imagining that you are on a school trip abroad;
b. a card from a friend of yours to you.

Telegrams seems to fall into two main categories: the urgent ones and the congratulatory ones. Neither type tends to be very long (since you pay for every word) and the art lies in putting across the message in as few words as possible. If your plane has been delayed in Paris and you will be arriving home on Sunday morning instead of on Saturday evening, you would probably write: PLANE DELAYED. ARRIVING SUNDAY MORNING. VERONICA. If your best friend is getting married and you can't attend the wedding you might telegraph: CONGRATULATIONS MAVIS AND GEORGE. YOU REALLY DESERVE EACH OTHER. SIDNEY.

3. Compose suitable telegrams for the following situations:
a. You have broken a leg on a ski-ing holiday in Switzerland and are returning home sooner than expected.
b. One of your old 'gang' is getting married. Send a telegram to him or her from a few old friends.
c. You arrived at Dover and realised that you had left your passport on the sideboard at home. You need it urgently. Give your address.
d. A new baby has just been born into the family and you send a telegram to your grandparents giving them the news.

4. Invent four interesting characters — young, old, male, female — and put each of them in an interesting place or situation, either at home or abroad. Write postcards and telegrams for each one of them, making the contents as varied as possible: dramatic, funny, sad, etc.

Spelling group
flippant   worshipped   handicapped   opportunity   opponent
opposite   oppose   disappoint   apply   happiness

30·Fiction and biography

There is a great deal one needs to know about a library before it can be used profitably. One needs to know how the books are numbered, classified and arranged on the shelves; where to look up information and how to use the many dictionaries that are available.

Most libraries use a classification system devised by Melvil Dewey (1851-1931) and named after him the Dewey Decimal Classification System. Under this system books are given a classification number ranging from 0 to 999 according to their subject. Almost every subject and sub-division of a subject can be classified under the Dewey system and the numbers go to several decimal places. If, therefore, you want a book on a rare subject like Horology (the art of making clocks), you could look up the Dewey number of Horology and go straight to the shelf where the book would be, since the books on the shelves are arranged in numerical order.

The card index is your most valuable assistance (apart from the librarian himself) in a library. Every book on the shelves is represented by a card which gives its subject, title, author, publisher and classification number. Thus, you can look up a book on the subject PUPPETRY, or one by the author ERNEST HEMINGWAY or one with the title THE OUTLINE OF HISTORY and be directed clearly to where it can be found.

Though the decimal classification is used for the majority of books in a library, there are one or two classes of book which are either exceptions or which have a special designation. These are:

i. **Fiction** (novels and stories). These books are not given numbers but are arranged on the shelves in alphabetical order under the surnames of the authors. The letter F is placed before the first three letters of the author's surname. Thus, if you wanted a novel by Charles Dickens you would look on the fiction shelves for F DIC. If you wanted a novel by Ian Fleming you would look for F FLE. Note that names beginning Mac, Mc and M' are all treated as if they were spelt Mac — and McInnes, therefore, comes before Mackintosh. The same principle is applied to names preceded by St., which are treated as if they were written out fully as Saint.

ii. **Biography and Autobiography.** These books may be classified in one of three ways: a). according to subject under the main scheme, when a biography of Beethoven, for instance, would come under MUSIC; b). placed in a separate class (920) and arranged according to occupation and interest within that class; or c). omitting a classification number and arranged alphabetically, according to the person being written about. A letter B is placed before the first three letters of the surname of the book's subject. Thus, a biography of Captain Scott written by Will Holwood would be marked B SCO. "My Autobiography", by Charles Chaplin, would be B CHA. Method c). is probably the most common way of arranging biography and autobiography in a library.

iii. **Reference books.** These books are given a Dewey number which is preceded by the letter R, indicating that they belong to the reference section of the library and may not be borrowed. They are dealt with in more detail in another workpaper.

1. The following books are either fiction, biography or autobiography. Write down the titles and after each one give the appropriate letters of classification.
   The Life of Mahatma Gandhi by Louis Fischer
   Memoirs of a Fox-hunting Man by Siegfried Sassoon
   The Jungle Book by Rudyard Kipling
   A Christmas Carol by Charles Dickens
   Lord of the Rings by J.R.R. Tolkien
   The Story of My Life by Helen Keller
   Cortez, Conqueror of Mexico by R. Syme
   Ice Station Zebra by Alistair Maclean
   The Circus is Coming by Noel Streatfield
   The Life of Samuel Johnson by James Boswell

Talking points
Fiction is probably the most popular form of reading. What stories or novels have you read recently? Give a short account of the story and the characters and then express your opinion of the book as a whole. Would you recommend it to someone else to read?
Who are today's best-selling authors? Why are they so popular? Does a good book always make a good film? Compare a book you have read with the film that was made from it. What changes took place?

What biographies or autobiographies have been read by members of the class? What attracted them to these books? Which tends to be more honest and truthful, the biography or the autobiography of a person? What do you think of books on the lives of pop stars?

Spelling group
diary   dairy   quite   quiet   goal   gaol   loose   lose   choose
chose

31·The Dewey System

Below are the main divisions in the Dewey classification system. There are, of course, numerous sub-divisions within each category and the details of these fill a book itself. For instance, the ten divisions from 530-539 deal with the following aspects of Physics: Mechanics, Liquids, Gases, Sound, Light, Heat, Electricity, Magnetism and Molecular Physics. Under Agriculture (630) there is The Farm (631) which is divided decimally into Farm Economics (631.1), Farm Buildings (631.2), Farm Machinery (631.3), Land, Soil (631.4) etc. It is thus possible under the Dewey system to place a book with an incredibly high degree of precision.

000	GENERAL WORKS	300	SOCIAL SCIENCES
010	Bibliography	310	Statistics
020	Library Science	320	Political Science
030	General cyclopaedias	330	Economics
040	General collections	340	Law
050	General periodicals	350	Public Administration
060	General societies: Museums	360	Social Welfare
070	Journalism	370	Education
080	Collected works	380	Commerce
090	Book rarities	390	Customs
100	PHILOSOPHY	400	LINGUISTICS
110	Metaphysics	410	Comparative
120	Metaphysical theories	420	English Language
130	Fields of psychology	430	German Germanic
140	Philosophical systems	440	French Provencal
150	Psychology	450	Italian Rumanian
160	Logic	460	Spanish Portuguese
170	Ethics	470	Latin Other Italic
180	Ancient philosophy	480	Greek Hellenic group
190	Modern philosophy	490	Other languages
200	RELIGION	500	PURE SCIENCE
210	Natural theology	510	Mathematics
220	Bible	520	Astronomy
230	Doctrinal theology	530	Physics
240	Devotional theology	540	Chemistry
250	Pastoral theology	550	Geology
260	Ecclesiastical theology	560	Palaeontology
270	Christian church history	570	Biology
280	Christian churches & sects	580	Botany
290	Non-Christian religions	590	Zoology

600	APPLIED SCIENCE	800	LITERATURE
610	Medicinal sciences	810	American
620	Engineering	820	English
630	Agriculture	830	German Germanic
640	Domestic economy	840	French Provencal
650	Commerce	850	Italian Romanian
660	Chemical technology	860	Spanish Portuguese
670	Manufactures	870	Latin Other Italic
680	Mechanic trades	880	Greek Hellenic group
690	Building construction	890	Other languages
700	ARTS & RECREATIONS	900	HISTORY
710	Landscape architecture	910	Geography
720	Architecture	920	Biography
730	Sculpture	930	Ancient world history
740	Drawing Decoration Art	940	Europe
750	Painting	950	Asia
760	Engraving	960	Africa
770	Photography	970	N. America
780	Music	980	S. America
790	Recreation	990	Oceania & Polar regions

1. Deducing what you can about the subject of the book from its title, give a Dewey classification number to each of the following:
A Guide to English Schools by Tyrrell Burgess; The Botanic Garden by E. Darwin; The Story of English Literature by Harry Bell; Where to Climb in the British Isles by E.C. Pyatt; The Holy Bible; The Solar System by Patrick White; A New Russian Grammar; Counterpoint and Harmony by E.C. Bairstow; Trampolining by D. Horne; A Decade of Revolution in France by R. Brinton; Opera by E. Dent; The Penguin Book of Japanese Verse; The Amateur Photographer by H. Nobes; A Guide to Modern Thought by C.E.M. Joad; The Glory that was Greece by J.C. Stobart; Greek in your Home by Caroline Hufford; copies of 'Punch'; Tibet's Great Yogi, Milarepa; Light, Mirrors and Lenses by F.E. Newing; Prehistoric Animals by K. Lombard.

2. Many of the subject categories in the Dewey classification system may be quite new to you. By using a dictionary and by questioning people who you think might know, find out what these words and phrases mean: book rarities, philosophy, logic, ethics, theology, sects, social sciences, linguistics, landscape architecture, engraving.

Spelling group
chaos   chorus   chasm   character   catechism   chronicle
chlorine   cholera   ache   choir

32·Reference books

There are numerous reference books in a public library and they are intended to be used to look up a specific piece of information, rather than read from cover to cover. They are usually thick, heavy tomes devoted to a particular subject and some of them are re-published annually to bring them up to date. The aim of this workpaper is to acquaint you with the better-known reference books on library sheves and to help you to decide which book to choose when you want to find out something.

1.   Below is a list of well-known reference books, excluding general encyclopaedias, which will be dealt with separately. Read through the titles and the brief description of the contents of each book, then answer question 2.

RELIGION
Dictionary of the Bible, J. Hastings. A full treatment of facts, concepts and beliefs.
Commentary on the Bible, A.S. Peake. Interpretations and comment on all the books in the Old and the New Testaments.
World Mythology. Brief accounts of all the major stories and characters in mythology of all civilizations.
Dictionary of Classical Mythology, J.E. Zimmerman. 2,000 entries on Greek and Roman mythology.

SOCIAL SCIENCES
Statistical Yearbook, published by the United Nations Organization. Statistics over a period of years relating to population, food production, schools etc. in most countries in the world.
Whitaker's Almanac. A quick reference book for information on statistics of population, members of parliament, public schools, etc.
Careers Encyclopaedia. Details of qualifications required, training, prospects, salaries on over 200 careers.
Stanley Gibbon's Simplified Stamp Catalogue. Published annually. Gives descriptions and prices of stamps.
Pears Cyclopaedia. A useful reference book for general knowledge, home and social affairs, such as medical matters, games, pets.
Everyman's Own Lawyer. The ordinary man's guide to the law.

LINGUISTICS
A Dictionary of Slang and Unconventional English. Gives the origin, usage and explanation of slang expressions, including oaths.
Roget's Thesaurus of English Words and Phrases. A treasury of words

connected in meaning, grouped under subject headings.

Concise Pronouncing Dictionary of British and American English, J. Windsor Lewis.

Modern English Usage, H.W. Fowler. The standard work on correct English style, grammar and usage. Errors analysed.

PURE SCIENCE

Chamber's Dictionary of Scientists, ed. A.V. Howard. In alphabetical sequence, information on scientists of all nations.

Chamber's Technical Dictionary. Definitions of 55,000 terms drawn from 100 branches of scientific and industrial activity.

Atlas of the Universe. Facts and maps on stellar and planetary systems.

Systematic Dictionary of Mammals of the World. Details of appearance, habitat, food, and breeding of all mammals.

British Birds. Details of nests, eggs, calls and habitat.

APPLIED SCIENCE

The Observer Books of: Ships, Railway Locomotives, Aircraft, Automobiles. Technical details, types, models, etc.

Jane's: World's Railways, World's Aircraft, World's Fighting Ships. Full details of all classes and types throughout the world.

THE ARTS AND RECREATION

Collins' Guide to English Parish Churches. Sir J. Betjeman. Descriptions of about 4,000 churches, with illustrations.

Dictionary of Arts and Artists. 1,400 entries, mainly biographical.

The Oxford Companion to Music. Opera plots, acoustics, musical instruments, biographies of composers.

Official Rules of Sports and Games. Covers rules of most major sports played today.

The Encyclopaedia of Athletics. Records of outstanding athletic events and biographies of famous athletes.

LITERATURE

Brewer's Dictionary of Phrase and Fable. Superstitions and customs, explanations of well-known phrases, lists of patron saints.

Everyman's Dictionary of Quotations and Proverbs.

The Oxford Companion to English Literature. Biographies of authors, plots of novels and plays, characters in fiction.

GEOGRAPHY AND HISTORY

Everyman's Dictionary of Dates. From earliest times to today.

Dictionary of Geography. Countries, major towns, technical terms, natural features.

Concise Oxford Dictionary of English Place-names. Origins of names.

Who's Who. An annual biographical dictionary of famous men and women.

Keesing's Contemporary Archives. A weekly diary of world events, drawn from news reports and official sources.

The Guinness Book of Records. World records in science, arts, sports, endurance — almost anything recordable.

2.   Let us assume that all the books listed on the two previous pages are available to you in the reference section of either your local public library or your school library. Below are some numbered items of information which you must look up in these reference books. Write the numbers in the margin of your exercise book and by each one put the title (or titles, since there may be more than one possibility) of the reference book(s) you would use to find out the information you want. To start off with the questions follow roughly the order of the books in the list, but they gradually diverge from this order and relate to books in any of the sections.

Of course the exercise need not be purely theoretical. If some of these books are in fact available to you, you could confirm that your answer is correct by looking up the answer in the book itself.

1.   Was the story in the Old Testament of Noah and the Flood based upon an historical event, or was it pure invention?
2.   You have been asked to find out what happened at the Transfiguration and to say what significance it has for Christian belief.
3.   What was the story of Icarus, who, according to Greek mythology, made himself wings and attempted to fly?
4.   You have seen an ivory carving of Hanuman, the Hindu monkey-god, and you wish to investigate further.
5.   You wish to know what the population of Great Britain was when the last census was taken.
6.   What special issues of stamps were made during last year?
7.   You are thinking of becoming a veterinary surgeon. What qualifications are necessary before you start a course of training?
8.   You have just bought a guinea-pig as a pet and you want to know its habits and what it eats.
9.   What is the law relating to the rent of controlled premises?
10.   You have to write a composition on thieves and you wish to collect words associated with thieves and thieving to help you with your preparation.
11.   In your reading you have come across certain colloquial expressions which baffle you. What is a 'flapdoodle'? What is meant by 'doing a moonlight flit'?
12.   What is the origin of the custom of giving eggs at Easter?
13.   There is often some confusion between the verb *to lie* and the verb *to lay*. What is the difference in their meaning and usage?

14. You have to find out for what modern scientific discovery Lord Rutherford was responsible.
15. What exactly is a superheterodyne receiver?
16. Where can the Blue Whale be found? What are its breeding habits and is it likely to survive?
17. You are doing a project on painters and you wish to look up some biographical details about Leonardo da Vinci.
18. You wish to look up the speed of the earliest aircraft.
19. A crossword puzzle clue asks you to complete the following quotation from Shakespeare: "All the perfumes of . . . will not sweeten this little hand."
20. You are studying the modern theatre and you want a short biography of Sir Lawrence Olivier.
21. You are writing an essay on the subject "Work" and you think some proverbs might give you one or two useful ideas.
22. Stoke Pero church is one of the smallest and most remote churches in England. Before visiting it you would like to learn something about it.
23. The night before the literature examination and you want a brief summary of the plots of 'Jane Eyre' and 'A Midsummer Night's Dream'.
24. For a current affairs debate you want to quote some examples of the violence in Northern Ireland during recent years.
25. What was the date of the battle of Waterloo?
26. You are interested in the records that were broken at the last Olympic Games.
27. What is the origin of the name of the town you live in?
28. What is the longest time a person has held his breath under water?
29. You are doing a project on writers of the 20th century and you wish to get some biographical details of H.G. Wells.
30. How were rift valleys formed?
31. What were the religious beliefs and practices of the Essenes, a religious sect existing at the time of Christ?
32. How do you pronounce the word *comparable*? Is the stress on the first or on the second syllable?
33. You intend to give a talk on astronomy and you would like to have some figures for the distances of the planets from the sun.
34. What are the main instruments in the woodwind section of an orchestra?
35. Which country in Europe produced the most wheat over a five-year period during the past decade?

Spelling group
factory   history   memory   oratory   theory   ivory   obligatory
territory   contradictory   category

33·General encyclopaedias

General encyclopaedias will be one of the chief sources of reference in a library, the advantage of them being that within the covers of a comparatively small set of books you can find information on a vast range of topics. There are also sets of encyclopaedias — and even single volumes — which deal with knowledge on a specific subject, such as religion, parliament or science; but this workpaper will confine itself to general encyclopaedias, of which there are usually sets in most schools.

It is common practice for articles in encyclopaedias to be arranged alphabetically, from A in the first volume to Z in the last volume and on the spine of each volume you will see printed the relevant letters, showing the distribution of articles. For instance, on Volume 7 of the *Encyclopaedia Britannica* there is:

DAMASCU - EDUC

This means that within that volume are all the subjects within that alphabetical range. Thus, if you wanted to look up DRAINAGE or EDINBURGH, this would be the volume to use.

Some encyclopaedias — *the Oxford Junior Encyclopaedia*, for instance — devote one volume to a specific aspect of knowledge, though the topics within that volume are arranged alphabetically. Thus, the *Oxford Junior, Volume 5* is entitled 'Great Lives' and in it you will find biographies of famous men and women arranged in alphabetical order.

With every set of encyclopaedias there is an index volume, which gives a list of all the topics covered and the particular volume in which the articles appear, including the page number. In the index volume of the *Children's Britannica* there is the following entry:

COINS AND COIN COLLECTING coins: tokens used in trade. The first true coins; how coins used to be made; hints for the collector 3-280b; 8-280b; alloy 1-139b; Britannia 2-309a; bronze 2-333a; copper 3-352a; gold 5-106a; threepenny pieces 10-84a; treasure trove 10-173b; tricks with coins 10-182a; pictures 3-281; coining press and coins, pictures 8-282.

The first number in each group of figures refers to the volume, the second number to the page in that volume and the letter a or b refers to the column on the page. Thus, if you wanted to look up some coin tricks you would go to page 182 in Volume 10. If you wish to refer to a sub-division of a main subject, it is always best to consult the Index first under the main heading.

You will probably be able to consult some of the following encyclopaedias either in your school library or in a public library:

The World Book Encyclopaedia: twelve volumes, with two additional volumes on the British Isles. An ideal encyclopaedia for schools.
Chamber's Encyclopaedia: specialises in British background material. Volume 15 contains general index and atlas.
Children's Britannica: arranged alphabetically with entries on popular and unusual topics which appeal to school pupils. Twelve volumes.
The New Book of Knowledge: twenty-four volumes, American in origin and having, therefore, an emphasis on American life and institutions.
The Oxford Junior Encyclopaedia: each volume deals with a specific category of knowledge: I Mankind, II Natural History, III The Universe, IV Communications, V Great Lives, VI Farming and Fisheries, VII Industry and Commerce, VIII Engineering, IX Recreations, X Law and Order, XI The Home, XII The Arts.
The Encyclopaedia Britannica: now published in three versions, from an abbreviated one to a very detailed one. The previous editions were in twenty-four volumes, including an Index and an Atlas. The entries range widely over many advanced subjects and it has been described as 'a comprehensive survey of universal knowledge'. It is rather too erudite, however, for the average school pupil.

The work arising from this description of encyclopaedias is to give you some practice at using the books themselves so that you will not be at a loss when you have to consult them, either for your own interest or for research and projects in a school subject.

Either: Choose a subject that you are interested in or something that in the past has appealed to you, but about which you know comparatively little. Look up the information an encyclopaedia gives on it. Make some notes, then either write them up in the form of an essay or make them the basis for a short talk to the class.

Or: Find out what an encyclopaedia has to say on one of the topics on the following pages. Write down the information in note form, then use the notes as the basis for an essay or a short talk in class.

If these particular encyclopaedias are not in your library, select a topic and look for it in any encyclopaedia that is available.

The World Book Encyclopaedia
Volume 1 Aeroplanes Archery
Volume 2 Ballet Butterflies
Volume 3 Capital Punishment Cowboys Chess
Volume 4 Divine Right of Kings Dominoes Eagles
Volume 5 Dates in film history Unusual fish Association Football

Volume 6 Hannibal   Holidays
Volume 7 Jazz   Jousting   Helen Keller
Volume 8 Magna Carta   Matches   Mercury
Volume 9 Outlaws   Pearls   Pompeii
Volume 10 Rockets   Roller skating
Volume 11 Solomon   Space Travel
Volume 12 Tides   Treasure-hunting   Duke of Wellington

Chamber's Encyclopaedia
Volume 1 The Acropolis   Arms and Armour   Mark Antony
Volume 2 Bayeux Tapestry   Bees   Bells   Bird Song
Volume 3 Cats   Cinema   Columbus   Circuses and travelling shows
Volume 4 Costumes through the ages   Cookery   Crowns
Volume 5 Electric power   Eskimos   Faith Healing   Festivals
Volume 6 Gangsters   Fungi   Greek Art
Volume 7 Homer   Horse racing   Infants and children
Volume 8 Jewish law   Lawrence of Arabia
Volume 9 Measures   Michaelangelo   Superstitions regarding the
          Moon
Volume 10 Nomads   Numismatics   Pigs
Volume 11 Early railways   Printing   Race   Rome
Volume 12 G.B. Shaw   Sharks   Scottish Literature
Volume 13 Spiritualism   Stars   Submarines   Swimming
Volume 14 United States   Queen Victoria   Water   Witchcraft

Children's Britannica
Volume 1 Adam and Eve   Alfred the Great   Animal behaviour
Volume 2 Balloons   Long Barrows   Boxing   Beetles   Bats
Volume 3 Camping   Cannibals   Lewis Carroll   Cosmetics
          Scottish clans   Camouflage   Christmas Customs
Volume 4 Detectives   Dolls   Eclipses   Fingerprints   Earthquakes
Volume 5 Gipsies   Girl Guides   Gymnastics   Galileo
Volume 6 Marathon   Monks and Friars   Motor Cycles   Judo
Volume 7 Olympic Games   Otter hunting   Pancake Day
          Pigeons   Party Games   Poisons
Volume 8 Radar   The Red Cross   Riddles   Royal Family
Volume 9 William Shakespeare   Smugglers   Speedway Racing
Volume 10 Tobacco   Underground Railways   Trinidad
          Television   Ventriloquism   Vandals   Van Gogh

New Book of Knowledge
Volume 1 Animated cartoons   African Music   Arabian Nights
Volume 2 Beavers   Boy Scouts   Ballooning   Basketball   Books
Volume 3 Cats   Camping   Circuses   China   Ceylon
Volume 4 Charles Dickens   Deserts   Dance music

Volume 5 Earthquakes Albert Einstein Environment
Volume 6 First Aid France in the Second World War Fencing
Volume 7 Galileo Guitars Genetics Gemstones Gliders
Volume 8 Hitler Hi-fi and stereo Health Hats Horse riding
Volume 9 Illuminated Manuscripts Islam Ice cream Ice skating
Volume 10 Jerusalem Jokes and Riddles Making a kite
Volume 11 Lighthouses Joseph Lister Legends
Volume 12 The Mayflower History of Medicine Music of the
           Middle Ages
Volume 13 Negro Spirituals Richard M. Nixon Negro history
Volume 14 Optical illusions Olympic Games Oceanography
Volume 15 Penguins Medicinal plants Planetariums Printing
Volume 16 Sir Walter Raleigh Prison life Ranch life Rock music
Volume 17 Soccer Scandinavian countries Shakespeare Sun
Volume 18 Thunder and lightning Tools Trees Tides Tennis
Volume 19 The Universe Ventriloquism Vikings Volcanoes
Volume 20 Wedding costumes Water pollution Watches Weather

Oxford Junior Encyclopaedia

I	Indians Giants Miracles	VII	Craft Guilds Gold Mining
II	Deer Gulls Salmon	VIII	Machines Tools
	Monkeys	IX	Football Ballet Folk Dancing
III	Astronomy Weather	X	Old Bailey Armed Forces
IV	Balloons Bridges Gliders	XI	Embroidery Nursing
V	Gandhi Churchill Hitler		Cookery
VI	Herbs Traps and snares	XII	Art Architecture

Encyclopaedia Britannica (24-volume edition)

1	Amphitheatres	13	Knighthood
2	Armoured trains	14	Livingstone
3	Battleships Beds	15	History of Mirrors
4	Brides: customs and ceremonies	16	Niagara Falls
5	Christmas customs	17	Mrs Pankhurst
6	Conjuring	18	Polo
7	Diamond mining Guide dogs	19	Strong-rooms
8	Elephants	20	Sleep
9	Fasting	21	Stars
10	Origins of golf	22	Titanic
11	Head-hunting	23	Witchcraft
12	Jackdaws		

Spelling group
league fatigue intrigue plague vogue vague rogue morgue
harangue **fugue**

34·Quiz questions

This workpaper involves a visit to a library where you will need to consult a number of reference books. The aim is not so much to test your knowledge as your ability to discover where the knowledge can be found. You will have to decide carefully which book of reference will give the quickest access to the information you want. Do not go immediately to the encyclopaedias. There are dictionaries on specific subjects that might be more helpful to you. If you want to look up a date, you would use the 'Dictionary of Dates'; if you want to look up a proverb, you would use the 'Dictionary of Proverbs'; if you want information on literature, you would use 'The Oxford Companion to English Literature' — and so on. If you do have to consult an encyclo-paedia, you can save time by looking up the Index volume first.

Below is a list of questions on a wide range of subjects and you are required to find the answers to some of these questions by referring to the relevant books. When this has been done, the questions will be asked in the form of a quiz, which can be arranged in one of several ways:

a.   the class is split into two main teams, A and B, which are themselves split into sub-teams of three or four pupils. The questions are divided equally amongst the sub-teams, who gain points for the main team if they answer correctly in the quiz;

b.   the questions are divided equally amonst the pupils in the class and the quiz is conducted on an individual basis;

c.   teams are chosen and the team members are free to select any number of questions from the list and may, if they wish, specialise in answering on a particular type of question.

All questions should be answered from memory.

1.   What was the date of the Massacre of Glencoe?
2.   What is the Palatine Guard?
3.   For what work in science was Sir Alexander Fleming renowned?
4.   Complete the quotations from George Bernard Shaw:
         All great truths being as . . .
5.   Into which sea does the River Volga flow?
6.   What musical instrument did Paganini play?
7.   Complete the proverb:
         Small sorrows speak; great sorrows . . .
8.   What was the date of the building of Hadrian's Wall?
9.   Who founded the religion of Islam?
10.   Who was Man Friday?

11. Who holds the record for the fastest crossing of the Atlantic alone in a boat?
12. What is the origin of the word 'Saturday'?
13. What was the Black Death?
14. Who painted the ceiling of the Sistine Chapel in Rome?
15. What exactly is cork?
16. What discovery was made by Alfred Nobel?
17. What is a Nobel Prize?
18. Into which sea does the Zambesi flow?
19. Complete the quotation from Lord Byron:
    Happiness was born . . .
20. Explain why it is necessary to have a leap year.
21. Who was the first astronaut to land on the moon?
22. What, apart from being a drink, is a 'gin'?
23. What is caviare?
24. Who was Inigo Jones and what was he famous for?
25. What is so special about the phoenix?
26. What is the astronomer's name for the dog-star?
27. What is the correct name for a water-rat?
28. Where is the Isle of Dogs?
29. Who are the four British patron saints and which country does each represent?
30. What is the Monday Club?
31. What is the origin of the name 'Christopher'?
32. What is the anatomical name for a) the shoulder blade and b) the collar bone?
33. Explain how aluminium is made.
34. What ceremonial function is performed by Black Rod?
35. What are the main ingredients of mead?
36. How was a toga worn?
37. The Serpentine in Hyde Park is formed from which dammed river?
38. Where in London is Sherlock Holmes supposed to have lived?
39. Which country was the first to introduce a national anthem?
40. What was a 'blue stocking'?
41. What happens in Islamic countries during the month of Ramadan?
42. In which year was Abraham Lincoln assassinated?
43. How would you wear a cummerbund?
44. Complete the quotation from Dr. Samuel Johnson:
    No man but a blockhead ever wrote except for . . .
45. What characterised the Copernican system in astronomy?
46. Where was the legendary land of Lyonesse?
47. What does 'dead men' mean in the song:
    Down among the dead men, let him lie?
48. What is Bombay Duck?

49. Who holds the record for bearing the most children?
50. What do we commemmorate on Easter Sunday?
51. What was the Minotaur and how was it slain?
52. What was Hitler's real name?
53. What pen-name did Charlotte Bronte use when she first published her novels?
54. What was the Roman name of St. Albans?
55. Where would you look for the statue of Peter Pan in London?
56. Which fish do you not catch when you are coarse fishing?
57. What is a haggis?
58. Gulliver travelled to Laputa on one of his voyages. Where was it?
59. What was the custom of 'suttee', which was once practised in India?
60. What is unusual about the Trappist order of monks?
61. Who was Tutankhamon?
62. What is the motto of the Royal Family?
63. Where would you go to see 'The Last Supper' by Leonardo da Vinci?
64. Who was Flora Macdonald?
65. What was Pestalozzi's nationality and profession?
66. In what way was Napoleon connected with 'the whiff of grapeshot'?
67. What was the Ptolemaic system in astronomy?
68. Jonathan Swift invented the 'Houyhnhnms'. What were they?
69. In which two islands did Napoleon spend his exile?
70. 'Das Capital' became the basis of which political ideology?
71. When did Brazil win the World Cup and with what score?
72. What is important about the DNA molecule?
73. On which railway line did Locomotion 1 first run?
74. What would you expect to see if you visited the Lascaux caves?
75. What would you be seeing if you were looking at 'The Thinker'?
76. What does the theorem of Pythagoras state?
77. What happened at the Boston Tea-party?
78. What is the better-known name of Charles Lutwidge Dodgson?
79. How did Britain come to own the Suez Canal?
80. What is Archimedes' principle in physics?
81. What happens at The Maltings, Suffolk?
82. Why are clouds formed?
83. Who was fighting whom in the Boer War?
84. What kind of entertainment was a 'masque'?
85. Why were the medieval alchemists seeking the 'philospher's stone'?
86. What is the meaning of the initials DC after the name Washington?
87. What theatrical presentation would you see at Oberammergau?
88. On which river are the Victoria Falls?

89. How did Socrates, the Greek philosopher, die?
90. What is a clepsydra?
91. Which theatrical character was the model for Mr. Punch?
92. How did Jesse James die?
93. The Pope is said to be the successor to which of the Apostles?
94. For what is La Scala in Milan famous?
95. What was Röntgen's famous discovery in 1895?
96. William Webb Ellis was responsible for beginning which game?
97. What would you expect to witness in the Colosseum after 80 A.D.?
98. Who was the first Secretary General of the United Nations?
99. In which French novel would you meet Quasimodo?
100. What was the Book of Kells and where is it now?
101. What was Launcelot Brown's other name and what was his profession?
102. Who built the Taj Mahal and for what purpose?
103. Which German doctor is associated with Lambarene?
104. Who was Alexander the Great's tutor?
105. What was a 'bootlegger'?
106. Why did Gandhi make salt from sea water?
107. Who was the first person to reach the South Pole?
108. What do cirrus clouds look like?
109. What connects the names Diaghilev and Nijinsky?
110. What event in British history occurred in 1603?
111. Which six countries have a common border with Austria?
112. What are the names of the nine planets in the solar system?
113. What was Charles Darwin's most famous publication?
114. How did the Tarantula spider get its name?
115. Define a mammal.
116. What is the Hippocratic Oath?
117. What is an ungulate?
118. 'Moby Dick' is the title of a book. What does it refer to?
119. What was an orrery and how did it get its name?
120. What shape is an elipsoid?
121. How does a stalactite differ from a stalagmite?
122. Which two countries derive their names from Amerigo Vespucci?
123. Which are the two land-locked countries of South America?
124. Name the Seven Deadly Sins.
125. Which architect designed the National Theatre?

Spelling group
potatoes   tomatoes   negroes   volcanoes   heroes   echoes
grottoes   torpedoes   mosquitoes   cargoes

35·Using a dictionary

The words in a dictionary are arranged in alphabetical order and it is comparatively easy to find the word you want. But is the definition that follows the word the one you want? English words have a habit of changing their meaning whilst retaining their spelling and before choosing a definition from a dictionary you should check that it makes sense when substituted for the original word in the text. For instance, let us assume that you came across the following sentence in a book:

Elsie used to fritter away her time when she was on holiday.
You are uncertain of the meaning of *fritter* and you look it up in a dictionary. One definition reads: *piece of fried batter often containing fruit.* You wonder what Elsie was up to during her holidays — was she cooking all day? The answer is that *fritter* in the sentence is a verb meaning *to throw away on divided aims,* whilst the *fritter* you have selected from the dictionary is a noun with a totally different meaning.

1.   In order to get some practice at distinguishing definitions of verbs and nouns with identical spelling but with different meanings, find in your dictionary two dissimilar definitions of the following words a). as verbs and b). as nouns:

    fray   hold   fence   train   boom   steer   watch   check
    blind   founder   book   peer

2.   The following words used as nouns will be given more than one definition in the dictionary. Look up the words and write down two separate definitions:

    bark   foot   date   painter   bull   pinion   kite   elder
    cosmos   jumper   fur   punch

3.   The words in italics in the following phrases can carry more than one meaning, but obviously one meaning is applicable whilst another is not. Find the definition that seems to make sense when substituted for the word in the phrase and write it down after the phrase itself.

    the *sound* led into the lake
    a toolmaker's *jig*
    the *foil* used in fencing
    the *hind* who works on a farm
    a *pound* in which animals are kept
    a *seal* of approval
    a *girdle* scone
    the *race* of a stream
    to *prime* a pump
    to read a *proof*

an official *recorder*
a meal of *pulse*

4. After the main entry for a word there are usually definitions of associated words. For instance, if you look up the verb *corrugate*, you will probably find also the noun *corrugation* under the same heading. Thus, if you are looking for the noun *initiation* you will be most likely to find it under the verb *initiate*. Similarly, the adverb *ingeniously* comes under the main entry *ingenious*, which is an adjective. It is useful, therefore, to be able to identify the part of speech of the word you are looking up and you should always explain a word by the same part of speech or its equivalent.

Below is a list of words with the part of speech given in brackets after each one. Look up in your dictionaries the associated parts of speech as indicated. Do not write out the definition.

stupid (adjective)   : look up the associated noun
translate (verb)   : look up the associated noun
optimism (noun)   : look up the associated adjective
endow (verb)   : look up the associated noun
translucent (adjective)   : look up the associated noun
hood (noun)   : look up the associated adjective
ruminate (verb)   : look up the associated noun
legend (noun)   : look up the associated adjective
pitiful (adjective)   : look up the associated adverb
radiate (verb)   : look up the associated noun

5. Read the following passage and for the words in italics write down a word or phrase equivalent in meaning and of the same part of speech. Look out for words with more than one meaning and select the definition that makes sense when substituted for the original word in the text.

Dr. Minchin was soft-handed, pale-complexioned, and of rounded outline, not to be *distinguished* from a mild clergyman in appearance: whereas Dr. Sprague was *superfluously* tall; his trousers got creased at the knees, and showed an excess of boot at a time when straps seemed necessary to any dignitary of *bearing*; you heard him go in and out, and up and down, as if he had come to see after the roofing. In short, he had weight, and might be expected to *grapple* with a disease and *throw* it; while Dr. Minchin might be better able to detect it lurking and to *circumvent* it. They enjoyed about equally the mysterious *privilege* of medical reputation, and concealed with much *etiquette* their contempt for each other's skill. Regarding themselves as Middlemarch institutions, they were ready to combine against all *innovators*, and against non-professionals given to interference.

Spelling group
admirable   desirable   durable   excitable   lovable   valuable
changeable   noticeable   marriageable   saleable

36·The beginnings of English

English is probably the most widely known and used language in the world. It is characterised by its wide vocabulary and its capacity to express fine shades of meaning. Many languages have contributed to the language we now call 'English' and even to this day new words are being added and the language is continually developing in new directions.

To study the growth of English we must look at the history of Britain and begin with the Celts who came to these islands from the mainland of Europe thousands of years ago as part of a vast migration of peoples from Central Asia. Their language — not surprisingly — was Celtic, but it was not destined to have very much influence on what was later to become 'English', and because the Celts were driven to the north and west by invaders the Celtic language survived only in these areas. It was spoken in Cornwall till the seventeenth century and it is still spoken in parts of Wales and Scotland today. A mere handful of Celtic words exist in modern English (*bard, bog, glen, galore, bannock, dun*, for instance), but many place-names are derived from Celtic. Thames, London and York are names that have their origin in Celtic and various Celtic words for 'river, water' are preserved in the names Avon, Exe, Usk and Ouse.

The Romans, led by Julius Caesar, invaded Britain in 55 B.C. and brought with them their own language, Latin, which, like Celtic, was of Indo-European origin. During this period both Latin and Celtic were spoken in Britain. The Roman occupation lasted for 400 years, yet hardly any Latin words came into English from this time. Of the few that did, the most common was *castra*, meaning 'camp' and it appears in the names of towns such as Chester, Lancaster and Gloucester. Thus, when the Romans left Britain to return to the defence of their empire, the Latin language virtually returned with them.

The English language, in fact, dates from the 5th century when the country was invaded by the Angles, Saxons and Jutes, who came from what is now North Germany. When they were not fighting, they were farmers and they took over all the good farming land. Some of the Celts became slaves and others migrated to Ireland and Wales where Celtic continued to be spoken. The language of the invaders was called 'Anglo-Saxon' and it was the principal language spoken in England for more than 500 years. It forms the basic vocabulary of English, the simplest words used for everyday objects, needs and relationships. For example: members of a family (*father, mother, son, daughter*), parts of the body (*head, eye, heart, foot, arm*), staple foods (*bread, oats, barley, wheat*), the cardinal numbers up to a thousand and the verbs *be, have, do, shall* and *will*. So basic and elementary is the vocabulary deriving from Anglo-Saxon that even to this day the words used by a young child up to the time when he learns to read are predominantly Anglo-Saxon.

In the ninth and tenth centuries there occurred the invasions by the Danes and the Vikings and they brought with them a language called Old Norse, which, like Anglo-Saxon, was a branch of the language spoken throughout Europe called Teutonic. The two languages existed in England simultaneously, with Old Norse prevailing in the northern half of the country where the Danes had chiefly settled and Anglo-Saxon in the south where the Angles, Saxons and Jutes had settled. For a time there was a certain amount of rivalry betwen the two languages. If there was a word in Old Norse and a word in Anglo-Saxon to describe the same thing, which word would be chosen? Often both words were retained and it is for this reason that we get certain synonyms in English, such as: *raise/rear, craft/skill*. Eventually, however, the two languages were fused together and became known as 'Old English', though it was not a standard language for the whole country. Dialects developed in the regions according to whether Danes or Anglo-Saxons predominated.

1. What was the first language to be spoken in Britain?
2. Can you explain why Celtic is spoken in certain parts of Wales today?
3. Can you explain why 80% of the place-names in Cornwall are of Celtic origin, while only 2% of the place-names in Suffolk are from Celtic?
4. What Celtic words are recognised by English-speakers today?
5. What other English towns and cities derive part of their name from the Latin word *castra*?
6. Why do we date the English language only from the fifth century?
7. Which language can be said to form the basis of English?
8. What language was spoken by a). Angles, Saxons and Jutes; b). the Danes? From what common European language were they derived,
9. Do a diagrammatic representation of the development of Old English from Teutonic by showing it as a family tree.
10. Can you explain the existence in English of the following pairs of synonyms? *hide/skin, sick/ill*.
11. Explain how dialects began to arise in this country.
12. Make a collection of dialect words and expressions.

Spelling group
gnat gnash design resign consignment neigh foreigner
campaign assign benign

37·The French influence

After the invasion of Britain by the Danes the country was at peace for some hundreds of years and Old English became well established. In 1066, however, William the Conqueror led the Norman invasion and a new upheaval began in the English language. The Normans became the government officials, the lawyers, the big landowners and the wealthy traders. They spoke French and they had no intention of learning Old English, the language used by the Anglo-Saxons, who were now a subject people. French, therefore, became the language of business, administration and the professions and was the official language of England for three hundred years. Old English was still used, but mainly for conversation and by the peasantry. As Latin was also used in the church and in schools, it meant that there were three languages operating in England at this time.

Language, however, never stands still and gradually, between 1066 and 1350 there was a fusion between Norman French and Old English which produced a language that was later called **Middle English.** This new language retained the basic structure and vocabulary of Old English and added to it a vast range of words that reflected the customs and culture introduced into England by the Norman invaders. In particular, words connected with food, government, war, trade and rank were added to the English: words such as *master, servant, dinner, supper, battle, tower, war, castle, justice, count;* and though the Old English words for animals (*cow, sheep, swine, deer*) continued to be used, the French names were used when these animals appeared on the table as cooked meat (*beef, mutton, pork, venison*). Often a French word would be added when there was an existing English word of the same meaning and the two words would exist side-by-side until gradually the meanings began to change and take on a different emphasis. Examples of this are *help, weak* and *work*, which come from Old English, and *aid, feeble* and *labour*, which come from French. From the overlapping of the two languages English acquired the vast number of synonyms which enable it to express such fine shades of meaning.

As the 'invaders' lost contact with France itself (in 1204 King John lost Normandy and the two countries were separated politically) the Norman barons eventually thought of England as 'home', they dropped French as a separate language and began to accept the new Middle English as their native tongue. In 1349 English was reinstated in the schools and in 1362 the Chancellor's speech opening parliament was, for the first time, delivered in English instead of in French. The same parliament forbade the use of French in the law courts on the grounds that "French is much unknown". After three centuries, therefore, English had triumphed as the predominant language of this country and of the many dialects spoken, the dialect of the East Midlands, spoken in and around London, became recognised as the standard one and formed the basis of modern English. A further stimulus to the new language was given by Geoffrey Chaucer (1340-1400), who used English for his set of stories entitled *The Canterbury Tales*, one of the landmarks of both English language and literature.

1.a. Which language was spoken in England before the Norman invasion?

b. What three languages were used after the Norman invasion and which classes of people used them?

c. What reasons were there for English, rather than French, becoming the predominant language?

d. Explain why the following words should be introduced into England at the time of the Conquest: a) banquet b) viscount c) veal d) curfew.

2. The following list contains pairs of synonyms, one word of each pair from French, the other from Old English. Put the words into pairs and, if possible, say which language each word comes from:

cure, meet, power, assemble, ancient, hearty, sell, love, cordial, heal, sharp, lord, vend, charity, might, odour, old, sire, poignant, smell.

3. Below are pairs of synonyms: one word from French, one from Old English. Though they may originally have been interchangeable, they now have slightly different meanings or applications. Discuss the differences.

ask, demand   answer, reply   house, mansion   ghost, spirit
room, chamber   shun, avoid   seethe, boil   body, corpse

4. The stream of French words that came into English after 1066 is unbroken today and modern English contains many expressions that are not only French in origin but which have retained their French form and spelling. Some examples are given below. Match the French expressions in **a.** with their English equivalents in **b.**

a. nom de plume, bête noire coup d' état, fait accompli, par excellence, dénouement, rendezvous, bon voyage, début, née.

b. pleasant journey, pen-name, a person one specially dislikes, something already done and unable to be changed, without equal, a meeting place, sudden and revolutionary change of government, the unravelling of the plot in a play or novel, born, first appearance.

Spelling group

coup d' état, fait accompli, rendezvous, table d'hôte, grand prix, début, nom de plume, menu, bon voyage, au revoir

38·The Renaissance

The main changes in the language of Britain had occurred through the invasions: the Romans, the Angles, Saxons and Jutes, the Danes and finally the Normans. After 1066, however, the invasions ceased and the English language developed more through literary influences than through conquest.

During the 15th and 16th centuries there was a great upsurge in learning throughout Europe. Men's minds seemed to develop a new inquisitiveness, their skills and energies sought new outlets. Daring voyages were undertaken, exciting scientific discoveries were made, new techniques in art and architecture were explored, new philosophies were expounded; and underpinning all this was a renewed interest in the language, learning and culture of the Greek and Roman civilizations. The movement was eventually called 'The Renaissance' (meaning 're-birth'), since it was a re-birth of interest in the great classical periods of European history. The effect of this revival of learning on the English language was considerable. New words began to flow into English from Latin and Greek to express the new learning, a task for which the English of the fourteenth century was wholly inadequate. Words with which we are now so familiar, such as *education, experiment, investigate, protest* and *capacity,* are first introduced into our language. It has been estimated that at least 10,000 words were added to English during the Renaissance and their acceptance would cause very little difficulty since Latin and Greek were taught in most English schools. Shakespeare was one of the heaviest contributors and seems to have been the first writer to use such words as *dislocate, obscene, hot-blooded* and *long-haired.*

It mustn't be forgotten, however, that the language of the ordinary man was not at first influenced by the new 'literary' vocabulary. He continued to speak his local dialect with all its rich variations and only gradually, as the years went by, did the new words become part of his habitual speech.

It was during this period that the English language began to be standardized, for during the years after the Conquest there had been many dialects, each with its own spelling, pronunciation and grammatical forms. However, an event of great importance in the history of English took place in the year 1467: Caxton introduced the printing press into England and began a process which many a schoolboy and schoolgirl might have cause to regret — the fixing of English spelling, which up until that time had been a hit-or-miss affair. Caxton chose to print in the East Midland dialect, thus helping to establish it as the accepted language of the country. His standard spelling was quickly copied and the movement towards 'correctness' gathered momentum as reading became more widespread and written communication more common.

Another landmark in standardization was to occur in 1755 when Dr. Johnson produced his *Dictionary of the English Language*, the aim of which was to "fix the pronunciation, preserve the purity, ascertain the use and lengthen the duration of the English language". He wasn't able to do that, of course, and even to this day there is no undisputed authority which can say how *controversy* should be pronounced or whether *all right* is right and *alright* is wrong. Perhaps it is just as well. If Dr. Johnson had had his way he would have outlawed such 'low' words as *coax*, *frisky*, *shabby* and *fuss* from the language; but by popular consent they remained and English continued on its way.

1.a. What difference was there in the way English developed before and after the Conquest?
b. Why was there a flood of new words into English during the Renaissance?
c. What helped the new classical words to be absorbed into English?
d. What two important effects resulted from Caxton's introduction of printing into England?
e. What is a 'lexicographer'? Look up the derivation of the word.

2. Below is a list of Latin words and their meaning. Write down a modern English word that is derived from each of the Latin words.
dentis (tooth); aqua (water); porto (I carry); annus (year); urbs (city); liber (book); altus (high); terra (earth); corpus (body).

3. Below is a list of Greek words with their meaning. Write down the modern English words which are derived from the Greek.
anti (against); auto (self); aster (star); gramma (letter); pathos (feeling); therme (heat); demos (people); lithos (stone); mikros (small); phone (voice).

4. 'Logos' is the Greek word meaning 'word' or 'study'. Give the English words ending in -ology which have come from the following Greek words:
anthropos (man); chronos (time); ge (earth); phyche (mind); theos (god); bios (life); grapho (I write); cosmos (world); arkhaios (ancient); morphe (form, shape)).

5. Find the meaning of the following Latin phrases: et cetera, in camera, bona fide, alma mater, Corpus Christi, terra firma, status quo, post mortem, magnum opus, ad nauseam, persona non grata.

Spelling group

legible   illegible   responsible   intelligible   digestible   edible
admissible   credible   terrible   incomprehensible

39·English goes abroad

After the Renaissance the most important development in English came through the spread of the language to foreign countries. The movement began in the seventeenth century, reached a climax in the eighteenth, and the results are evident today, since nearly four times as many speakers of English exist on non-European soil as in Britain itself.

The first expansion came with the growth of the British Empire in Australia, New Zealand, South Africa and, in particular, North America, where today there are 200 million English-speaking people. Throughout the world there are about 300 million who speak English — approximately one out of every ten of the world's inhabitants.

English spread abroad, but it also acquired new words from the languages it came into contact with through trade, colonization and the growth of communication, though these words were few compared with the acquisitions from French, Latin and Greek. Words from a foreign language would usually represent a special skill possessed by the people who spoke that language. Thus, from the Dutch, who were highly skilled in commerce and sea-faring, we get *schooner, sloop, skipper, dock, smuggle, brandy* and *gin*. From the Italians, who excelled at music, we borrowed *piano, sonata, fantasia, tempo* and *crescendo*. Or the words might simply be the names of creatures, objects or products which were entirely new to the English and for which no English equivalent existed. Hence from Spanish and Portuguese: *rodeo, cockroach, cork, mosquito, sherry;* from German: *sauerkraut, poodle, nickel, cobalt, quartz;* from Hindustani: *polo, loot, dinghy, shampoo, bungalow, curry;* from Arabic and Persian: *algebra, syrup, alcohol, sofa, mattress, magazine*. These are but a few examples. We are still adding words to English from foreign languages, perhaps at a greater rate today than ever before.

The real growing point in the English language in recent times, however, has been the United States, where 'American' English has acquired a vast new vocabulary created by a different physical background to that of England, changing social and industrial relations and inventions in all spheres of life. The mixture of immigrant races has also meant another influx of words from foreign languages ranging from Italian to Chinese. The American version of English was at first deplored as 'barbarous', threatening to destroy the purity of the English language, and even today there are people who can't bring themselves to use words like *kids* and *guys;* but we cannot deny the debt English owes to the United States for its renewed vitality. Our language would be less rich without such American words as *hitch-hike, highbrow, bulldoze* and such lively idioms as *to bark up the wrong tree, a chip on*

the shoulder, horse sense, stag party, dead beat, assembly line,
cooling-off period, take-home pay, white-collar worker, lockout, dark
horse, lame duck and *to sit on the fence.* The divergence between
English and American which began in the seventeenth century is now
beginning to slow down and the reasons for it are not difficult to find:
the increased contact between the countries through commerce, travel,
television, films, literature and politics developed a vocabulary that has
become increasingly common, though the flow of words towards
England has been greater than that from it.

1.a. What reason was there for the spread of English throughout the
   world?
 b. Give four reasons why English vocabulary has developed so rapidly
   in the United States in recent times.
 c. Give five examples from the passage above of American words
   dealing with industrial relations that are now common usage in
   Britain.
 d. The American spelling of certain words differs from the English
   spelling. How would an English writer spell the American: humor,
   theater, offense, program, traveler, favorite, center, check?
 e. Write a brief explanation of the following American idioms: stag
   party, dark horse, to sit on the fence, shotgun wedding, favourite
   son, highfalutin, caboodle, chip on one's shoulder.

2. Below is a list of 'foreign' words which are now generally used and
understood by English-speakers. From what you know about these
words and by consulting a dictionary if necessary, say which part of the
world and which language each comes from.

spaghetti	kimono	kibbutz	bolshevik ('bolshie')
boomerang	haiku	aria	tomahawk
blitz	pasta	patio	vodka
judo	wigwam	steppe	blitz

Can you think of other foreign words that have been introduced into
English, particularly connected with sport, food and dress?

3. Sometimes a word has a different meaning on each side of the
Atlantic; or English and American speakers will name the same object
differently. Can you say what the English equivalent is of these
American words?

sidewalk	suspenders	purse	subway	fall
elevator	movies	gas	thumb-tack	railroad
cookie	French fries	potato chips	schedule	math
fender	trashcan	candy	sick	automobile

Can you give some more examples of American English?

Spelling group
cheque antique physique plaque technique unique
delinquency picturesque bequeathe queue

40·The new vocabulary

If you were to ask a person in his fifties to imagine himself a youth again and to say whether, forty years ago, he would know what you were talking about if you used the words *blast-off, briefs, flyover* and *disco*, what do you think he would say? He would have to admit that he was baffled, that as a youth he had never heard of these words, and he would be right because at that time the words did not exist in the English language. Today, however, they are common words which most people know and sometimes use. There are many more words like them, the product of an age that has forged ahead in almost all directions and has needed a wider vocabulary to describe what it has encountered and produced.

Some of the words are newly created, others are not strictly new words but combinations of old words to convey a special meaning. Often the new vocabulary is so technical that it cannot be understood by the non-specialist and becomes an exclusive jargon; at other times it is simple and necessary for everyday life and becomes immediately accepted. The spread of new words has been helped by television, radio, books and magazines and the advertising that attaches to these media; and it is probably true to say that new words and expressions catch on more quickly today than they ever did in the past, though not all the words stay the course and become a permanent part of the language. Here are some examples of the newcomers to English, grouped under subject headings:

Science and technology: *count-down, launching pad, reactor, off-set litho, radar (ra*dio detection and ranging), *space probe, nylon, transistor, laser, videotape, reprographic, feed-back, automation;*
Clothes: *jeans, anorak, separates, tights, T-shirt, caftan, donkey jacket, poncho, sneakers, briefs, tank-top;*
Entertainment: *disc-jockey, pop-star, discotheque, quizmaster, science fiction, best-seller, movie, stereo, drag act;*
Travel and transport: *juggernaut, minicab, minibus, moped, scooter, articulated lorry, container transport, motel, air terminal, flight-path, underpass, subway, heliport, sliproad, motorway, multi-storey car park, parking meter, traffic warden;*
In the home: *deep-freeze, de-frost, kitchen unit, double-glazing, patio, loft-conversion, extractor, waste disposal unit, liquidize, blender;*
Society and politics: *Welfare State, fringe benefits, opinion poll, status symbol, pressure groups, environmentalist, preservationist, bomber, detainee, credit card, home help, senior citizen, Ms, chairperson;*
Education: *reluctant learner, integrated studies, team teaching, creative writing, teach-in, maladjusted, middle school, pastoral care, gifted*

pupil, course work, school counsellor, unclassified, resource centre.

1. There are fashions in words as there are in clothes. Some words are popular for a time and then are replaced by more expressive words; some words fall by the wayside because what they describe is no longer in common use; other words become socially or politically unacceptable and are replaced by something more discreet or attractive. Below are some words which, for one reason or another, have fallen behind in the verbal popularity stakes. Can you find out which words or phrases have replaced them?

wireless	mannequin	mad, insane	a dunce
a backward country	the rat catcher	undertaker	crooner
commercial traveller	charlady	barber	

2. Hyphenated words have been on the increase in recent years. Can you write a brief definition of the following examples?

in-fighting	a sit-in	a take-over bid	one-off
a phone-in	a walkie-talkie	a work-out	ex-works
ex-directory	lay-by	side-effects	drip-dry

3. Abbreviations or the initial letters of a group of words often grow into words in their own right. Give the meaning of the following and write out the word or expression in full:

hi-fi IQ   bra   STD   ESP pop DJ VAT   NATO   ITA

4. Popular music and all that goes with it has been responsible for introducing many new words into English and for giving some old ones an new twist. Typical of these words are *group* and *rock*, which had quite different meanings earlier in the century. What other words from the world of music are comparatively recent additions to English?

5. Slang and colloquial English change very rapidly. Who nowadays uses words like *swank, bigshot* and *spifflicate?* They were popular in their day, but have been replaced. Can you make a list of slang and colloquial expressions in common use today, starting with that odd little word, *OK?*

6. Compile your own list of new words. Look at newspapers, magazines of all kinds and at textbooks; ask people of your acquaintance if they know any words connected with their work which have been introduced in recent years. Find out the meaning and, if possible, the origin of the new words or expressions and introduce them under subject headings to the class.

Spelling group
independence   impatience   indolence   permanence   prominence
precedence   reverence   dependence   diligence   competence